Maggi

949.27

The
ANCIENT ROAD
Rediscovered

WHAT THE EARLY CHURCH KNEW...

M. JAMES JORDAN

©2014

The Ancient Road Rediscovered - by M. James Jordan
Published by Fatherheart Media 2014

PO Box 1039, Taupo, 3330, New Zealand
www.fatherheart.net

Printed in the USA/NZ

ISBN: 978-0-9941016-5-5

For other books, e-books, teaching, CD, DVD or MP3 of James Jordan please visit www.fatherheart.net/shop. Online international orders welcome. International shipping available.

FATHERHEART
MINISTRIES
www.fatherheart.net

Dedicated to the international Fatherheart Ministries family.

CONTENTS

Acknowledgements

This book has come into being as a result of many years of seeking the Lord for help and answers to the struggles that my wife Denise and I have been through together. It is usually the desperate heart that cries out to God the loudest. Most of the things written here have come to me by direct revelation. The chapter on The Two Trees came to Denise first and we have agreed to include it here as I see and teach it.

My thanks first and foremost go to Denise who has loved me beyond reason and been so patient with me over more than forty years we have walked together as we have learnt these things.

I also want to especially thank Stephen Hill who has put the longest hours searching many spoken messages and collating the salient points into intelligible text. His ability and concentration levels amaze me.

I am grateful to Alice Adams and Tom Carroll who have given of their effort and time with willing hearts. Alice for her copy-editing and proofreading work, and Tom for his work in design and presentation. Thank you.

I wish to acknowledge the wider family of Fatherheart Ministries around the world with whom I have lived in varying states of community life over the last seventeen years. In the stillness of this family life, I have found love and rest enough to 'see' things that I wouldn't have been able to see otherwise.

I am grateful to all of those who have had some part to play in my life over the years. My life is not only the product of the Holy Spirit's work in me but also the product of those who have walked with me. Even those who were seemingly against me at times have played a part in who I am now. All things have worked together for good for me and I am grateful for all the ways I have been ministered to by the Body of Christ.

The encouragement to get this material into book form has come from so many people in different places around the world. It is impossible to mention them all by name.

My hope is that the efforts of the many people who put this book together will be a joy to our Heavenly Father and a blessing to all those who take the time to read it. I submit it to you all dear brothers and sisters in the Body of Christ.

M. James Jordan

The Ancient Road

A few years ago I had a vision of a knight on a white horse dancing through a deep and ancient forest. During that vision, which I describe in detail in my book *Sonship*, it suddenly became clear to me that I was standing on an ancient road. Winding through the forest, it was almost invisible, being so overgrown with weeds and grass. But it was a road on which the Holy Spirit (represented by the white horse) was a frequent traveller. Amazingly, this road on which the white horse danced was *seldom used* by anyone else.

What is that ancient road and where does it come from? Equally importantly, where is that road going? To what destination is it headed?

I now wonder if the Gospel that most of us have been exposed to is actually, in the words of Paul in Galatians 1:6, 'another gospel.' Much of what we have heard has not really been good news. Thousands have stopped going to church because they no longer enjoy it. What is happening? What has gone wrong? My belief is that we have had a version of Christianity that claims to be good news but actually isn't. We have been so indoctrinated that even when we are burning out in our service to the Lord we still gasp that it is 'good news.' This is ludicrous. It just doesn't add up.

Many Christians have discovered that the kind of Gospel

they have assimilated has driven them into a striving, sweating spirituality that only leads to burnout and is energised by obligation, duty, guilt and condemnation. There is even so-called 'Christian' teaching on how to avoid burnout. How ridiculous is that! As if burnout is to be expected as a routine part of Christian life. Let me say very clearly: If you are on the road to burnout you are on the wrong road completely. There isn't a fine line between burnout and serving the Lord. There is a gaping chasm! Burnout comes from working in the power of the flesh - there is no argument about it! You *cannot* burn out if you are walking and working in the Spirit. Jesus said that His yoke is easy and His burden is light.

I do not believe there is any freedom, joy or rest except in the love of the Father. We have been living a Christianity that is handicapped by a lack of revelation of the Father. To put it simply, we have been living a Christianity based on two revelations; the revelation of Jesus as Saviour and Lord, and the revelation of the Holy Spirit's indwelling. This is like trying to balance on a two-legged stool. To put it another way, the foundation of our Christianity is incomplete. Something vital is missing. To date we have had only a conceptual understanding rather than a revelation of the Father. What is more, we have had a *flawed* understanding of who the Father is.

When the Holy Spirit hit Toronto in 1994 it heralded a new day in the Spirit. There was a new openness to the revelation of the Father. Prior to 1994, preaching about the Father, which I had been doing since 1979, was like trying to push water uphill with a rake. It just didn't take hold in people's hearts. With the exception of Youth With A Mission, who had invited Jack Winter to minister freely, my experience was that the revelation of the

Father had little or no impact. When the Holy Spirit hit Toronto however, that changed overnight. There was a climate change in the spiritual atmosphere around the world. Those who had been touched by what was happening in Toronto suddenly became open and hungry to know about the Father's love for them. That change was very obvious to me because I was one of the few who had been preaching about and walking in an experience of the Father's love. A watershed emerged in the history of the Church.

Twenty years have passed since then and it has been extraordinary to witness how God is revealing Himself as Father right across the globe. This revelation has reached every denomination and every stream within the Body of Christ and we are hearing testimonies of how it is reaching beyond the Church into the hearts of individuals from every level of society. Of course, not everyone who was touched by what happened in Toronto really grasped the true significance of it. Many people focused only on the physical effects of the presence of God in meetings.

I believe however, that as we look back, we will see that 1994 was the year when the revelation of the Father began to be reestablished in the Church. The year 1994 was the beginning of a new and significant era in the history of the Church. There was a mighty outpouring of the power of God then, which was wonderful. However, if you have a move of the Spirit without a revelation of the Word it will inevitably dissipate and eventually disappear. The Spirit and the Word must go together to build the Church. There is a revelation of the Word that has followed in the wake of the outpouring of the Spirit in Toronto. The river of the Spirit is also a river of revelation in the Word. Personally speaking, I have felt as if I have been standing in a river of revelation for the last twenty years. The revelation of the Word is coming forth in an increasingly fresh way. The centre of gravity in Christianity as we know it has shifted. The ancient road of Jesus and the Apostles is being rediscovered.

It is becoming very clear that the Christianity ahead of us is different from the Christianity behind us. What we are entering into is of a very different character to what we have known before. When this began to occur to me it made me realise what an incredible thing it was when Jack Winter got his original and quantum-leap revelation, that the love of the Father is a substance that can be imparted. Out of that watershed everything else within this revelation has come. It took us from the charismatic era to another era. It leapt from the era of the power and gifts of the Holy Spirit to the love of the Father that could be experienced. It was a huge leap - from what was only a *concept* that God loves you to the *experiencing* of Him *loving* you. It was not only a theological paradigm shift; it was a step beyond the limits of Christian experience. I believe *that* groundbreaking revelation has been the catalyst to usher in a new era of Christianity.

Now that we are beginning to experience the Father, we are seeing the Father on every page of the Bible. The whole Bible is becoming like a new book. When we receive revelation it sheds an entirely different light on our whole theology. Many sacred cows that we have held onto tightly are exposed in the light of new revelation. One man said to me after a meeting some time ago, "James, you have just driven a plough through my theology!" I thought that was a fair comment because I have had a plough driven through *my* theology as well.

This revelation of the Father is radically changing our

experience and understanding of Christianity. It is not that we are coming into anything new, however, for this is all throughout the Scriptures. The Bible is full of it and when you become awakened to it you see it everywhere. Then it takes courage to grow in it and hold onto it, even if you have to walk alone and those you fellowship with do not understand it. I always tell people who receive this revelation that they shouldn't be in any hurry to share it with others. It is better, rather, to grow in it until it starts spilling over the top of the vessel that you are. As you grow in it and enjoy it for yourself there will inevitably come a time when people will begin to notice something different about you. When they ask you then tell them - but not before! Don't feel the need to persuade people if they are not hearing you. If they don't hear it, it simply means that they *can't* hear it. Revelation is not something that can be forced down a person's throat. Knowledge can, but revelation is either grasped or it isn't. A person either gets a revelation or they don't. It is as simple as that.

As we have come to experience the love of the Father our perspective on many things is changing. One of these things, for example, is that the centrality of the heart becomes an issue of fundamental importance. When you are not experiencing love, all that you possess is mostly knowledge. But love can only be experienced in your heart. Your heart needs to be open to receive love. You can have a new teaching *about* love, but it takes an experience in your heart to receive the *actuality* of love. As we begin to experience Him loving us more and more, our hearts come into sharper focus. The condition of our heart is put under a magnifying glass and we begin to realise how important the heart really is.

As a result, we are finding that many things regarding how we understand Christianity are changing quite dynamically. This is the crux of it. It is not merely that your heart is important. The reality is that your heart is *vital*, because it is your heart that is changing. Knowledge is something that is of the mind but understanding is an issue of the heart. Many verses in the book of Proverbs speak about this. Let me give some advice to you. If you read something in the Scriptures and you do not understand it, you need to ask yourself whether there is something in your heart that is hindering you from not understanding it. You need to ask that question because understanding is an issue of the heart. Proverbs 14:6 states very clearly, "...knowledge is easy to him that understands." The Scriptures tell us continually to seek understanding because when you understand at a heart level then you will see and have clarity of knowledge.

In our relationship with God we relate to Him heart to heart. He doesn't look on outward appearances but He looks upon the heart. He Himself is a 'heart' person. Follow that to its logical conclusion: if He is looking at your heart and you are doing something for Him that doesn't come from your heart, He doesn't even notice it. We do so many things for God that are purely by rote. We can say grace before meals, for example, but many times it doesn't come from a heart that is genuinely thankful. I am not saying that you shouldn't say grace before meals, but if you are going to say it at all let it be an expression of your heart. If you do something towards God that is not out of your heart then it is just religiosity. If you desire to be a man or woman of God you are going to have to live your life towards Him from your heart. Of course you need to use your mind for many things in life, however, in all things pertaining to God the core issue is the heart.

In the Body of Christ we have struggled to understand many

things that are outside our sphere of revelation. One of our problems as human beings is that we have an inbuilt tendency to want mastery. We want to be able to master concepts, be it mathematics, golf, driving fast cars or even space exploration. There is something innate in us that wants to master life and be good at it. In the kingdom of God, however, there is more mystery than mastery. We have to come to terms with the fact that there will always be mystery. Our problem is that we want to master Christianity as well. We want to master the moving of the Holy Spirit. We want to get it down to a fine art that we are in control of and can make happen as we wish, but God cannot be mastered by us. The great adventure of Christianity is that we are going to keep discovering Him throughout eternity. We are going to keep exploring the unfolding mystery of who He is at greater and greater levels as He reveals more and more of Himself throughout eternity.

One thing that we do know about God is that He is love. We are coming into that revelation more and more - but there is still a lot more Scripture there than we have revelation of as yet. The Bible cannot be understood simply by intellectual study. It is a revelation of God and His dealings with mankind and can only be grasped when He shines light on it, when He reveals Himself in and through it. I believe that there is a lot more in the Bible than has yet come out of it because the Word of God endures forever and is eternal. You can read the Word and form opinions on it. One thing I can tell you is that you will get fed up with people's opinions on the Word. There are many arguments on the basis of opinion but when there is revelation it is no longer a matter of opinion or debate - it is truth! When you receive revelation, you possess knowledge at a much deeper level than mere opinion. You have experience as well as information.

We have a Bible in our hands that we have a *certain* amount of revelation on. That means, however, that there is a lot more Scripture that we have *not* got revelation on. What then happens is that we try to put together, from our study, a logical understanding of the things that we lack revelation on. We form doctrines out of our logical on-flow from revealed truth. We try to fill in the gaps because we want mastery. So much of our inherited theology is not revelatory but is speculative opinion; it is our biased thinking about particular issues. This is largely why there are doctrinal differences in the Body of Christ.

I came to a place in my life where I was weary of people's opinions on what the Scripture meant. I was equally weary of *my own* opinions. I realised that the Bible is not to be studied as a manual for Christian life and growth. The Bible is a place to meet God. You read the Bible to touch God, not to form opinions on what it means. Like prayer, it is a place where God can speak to you. There are people whose role is to study the original languages so that the meanings of the words are clear and sharp for us but that is a specific calling. It is not the basis of the faith-walk of the believer.

God gives revelation on things that we have not had revelation on before. When that happens most of the opinions that we have formed are blown away. We suddenly realise that our opinion on a particular issue was wrong. The problem is that we can be emotionally attached to our opinion and find it difficult to let go. If you are a pastor, you may well have been preaching that opinion for years and then God gives revelation on what it *really* means. You are then faced with having to throw away all those years of preaching and teaching. I had my theology neatly packaged in a box with a nice ribbon on it and now revelation has blown it apart! Fresh revelation takes you back to being a child once again. It forces you to begin all over again in your understanding. This can be difficult and humbling for those, like preachers or teachers, who have a personal investment or reputation surrounding their opinions.

This revelation of the Father's love is growing and blowing apart much of the stuff that we were convinced was right. But when we see the Lord, all our questions will be answered. The revealing of Him in His true nature will clear up every outstanding question. Christianity is based on nothing else but the revealing of who God really is. Reading words *about* Him is not what Christianity is. Revelation comes spirit to spirit.

When the doors of heaven open up, Peter (in Mt 16:16) sees the absolute reality of who Jesus is and blurts out, "You are the Christ the Son of the living God!" The building block of the Church is the revealing of who God is. When the Body of Christ begins to walk in the revelation of who God truly is then that ancient road that the Holy Spirit traverses on is found again.

This book is very different from my first book. This book is written as a prophetic message to the Body of Christ. The prophetic has a corrective character to it. It pulls down what is wrong and reestablishes the true. Much of the gospel that we have been taught has stolen joy, disempowered Christians and been the foundation for legalism to grow. It is no better than an Old Testament form of piety with the name of Christianity. It is very clear to me that the whole understanding of the mindset of Christianity has to shift so that it will begin to see the reassembling of that which Jesus died to give us.

I have written this book specifically for those who will be the communicators of the Gospel in the future. It is my hope and belief that we will see the authentic Gospel being preached; a Gospel that sets the captives free, that gives sight to the blind, that opens prison doors and that truly proclaims the favour of our God.

The book is divided into two main sections. The first section shows what the Gospel really is. It outlines some of the major paradigm shifts that the Holy Spirit has opened up, bringing a refreshing new perspective of what Christianity is really meant to be. The second part of the book then looks at the difference that this perspective makes in our Christian walk. If you come into a revelation and experience of the Gospel the fruit is very different from what the gospel of religion has produced.

This book is written from my heart, out of my own failure and brokenness, but also out of the wonderful rest and enjoyment of coming to know the Father's love for me!

PART ONE

CHAPTER ONE

~

The Two Trees

In his letter to the Galatians, the apostle Paul, after opening with his customary greeting, plunges straight in, getting directly to the point of why he is writing. Without pulling any punches, he writes the following words:

> *I marvel that you are turning away so soon from Him who called you in the grace of Christ to another gospel which is not another, but there are those who trouble you and want to pervert the Gospel of Christ.* – GALATIANS 1:6,7

Paul is making a striking statement here. He is addressing those who had become Christians under his preaching. He had established them in their faith and then left them to go elsewhere. After he departed, other teachers came among them, greatly influencing them. Paul, hearing about what had transpired in the aftermath of these other speakers, is compelled to write this letter.

He is amazed that they have put aside what he has taught them and have been corrupted by other teachers. The Galatians have believed that what they have heard is the Gospel but it is *not* the Gospel. Put simply, they have been deceived.

This letter from Paul must have been hard to swallow for these young believers. They had only known Paul briefly. They were doing the best they could do to grow in their new faith. With good intentions they received these other preachers who seemed to be nice, genuine people. I'm sure that everything the teachers said sounded good and right. These teachers stayed around longer than Paul had. They were made welcome in the Galatian church. No one could have suspected them of having anything less than the purest motives for what they taught and did.

But then the Christians in Galatia are contacted again by Paul who hits them with a broadside: "You have been led astray by these teachers that you have been listening to!" Notice that Paul doesn't question the sincerity of the believers in Galatia; he does not accuse them of sin or rebellion. They were trying to do the right thing. They weren't trying to corrupt the Gospel. They wanted to grow in their faith by listening to good teaching. But Paul insists, "These teachers have led you astray. They have *bewitched* you."

The question I put to you is this;

> *Is it possible for the same thing to happen to us? Do you believe it is just possible that the good teaching we have listened to has led us into a gospel that Paul would call "another" Gospel?*

The word 'gospel' means good news. I know for myself that much of what has been presented to me over the years of my Christian life has not turned out to be good news to me. Denise and I gave our lives to the Lord in 1972. We got filled with the Holy Spirit and for many years we tried to do the right thing, serving with all our energy. We longed to be everything that a Christian was meant to be. However, in 1988 we hit a wall and we burned out. We were completely exhausted emotionally, spiritually and physically. Denise and I have always done everything together with all of our hearts and we burned out together. Let me tell you - burning out in the service of the Lord is not all it is cracked up to be. For three solid months the tears were streaming down our faces. We didn't know why we were weeping. We were utterly spent! We felt that we had let God down. All of our effort to live the Christian life had ultimately led us into a deep, dark pit. It took us many years to recover.

It was a shock for me to look back on my Christian experience and realise that there had been little fun at all. Apart from the genuine experiences of being born again, baptised in water and baptised in the Spirit, Denise and I had adopted a form of Christianity that was ultimately not good news. It was completely devoid of any real enjoyment, any deep and wonderful joy! The recognition that I had not done anything that I actually enjoyed doing since becoming a Christian hit me with a jolt. At that point I had been a Christian for eighteen years and I had not done one single activity for sheer enjoyment in all that time. It had been a life of strong discipline, ardent zeal, sacrifices and hard work! It dawned on me that we had been living the opposite of good news. I am sure that many, many Christians identify with my description of the 'gospel' that we were believing and living.

TWO TREES IN THE GARDEN

What then is this false gospel that has deceived us? To answer this question we need to go back to the very beginning. Much of the revelation that the Lord has given us in our lives and ministry goes back to the beginning, back to the Garden of Eden. As we were slowly coming out of burnout, Denise and I began to suspect that something was very deeply amiss with what we, and indeed many other believers, were living in. A massive credibility gap existed between what the Bible spoke of as 'good news' and the reality that many Christians over the centuries had been living in. We were catching on to something that we couldn't find the words to adequately describe. Then, a few years ago, Denise was reading the opening chapters of Genesis and suddenly saw something, which has radically changed our perspective on life and ministry. What she saw has been a major paradigm shift and has brought us into a freedom that we often wondered was even possible.

To explore this let's begin by looking at Genesis 2:8-15:

> *The Lord God planted a garden eastward in Eden, and there He put the man whom He had formed. And out of the ground the Lord God made every tree grow that is pleasant to the sight and good for food. The Tree of Life was also in the midst of the garden, and the Tree of the Knowledge of Good and Evil.........Then the Lord God took the man and put him in the Garden of Eden to tend and keep it. And the Lord God commanded the man, saying, "Of every tree of the garden you may freely eat; but of the Tree of the Knowledge of Good and Evil you shall not eat, for in the day that you eat of it you shall surely die."*

We then read in the opening verses of Genesis 3:

> *Now the serpent was more cunning than any beast of the field which the Lord God had made. And he said to the woman, "Has God indeed said, 'You shall not eat of every tree of the garden'?" And the woman said to the serpent, "We may eat the fruit of the trees of the garden; but of the fruit of the tree which is in the midst of the garden, God has said, 'You shall not eat it, nor shall you touch it, lest you die.'"*

> *Then the serpent said to the woman, "You will not surely die. For God knows that in the day you eat of it **your eyes will be opened**, and you will be like God, knowing good and evil."*

> *So when the woman saw that the tree was good for food, that it was pleasant to the eyes, and a tree desirable to make one wise, she took of its fruit and ate. She also gave to her husband with her, and he ate. **Then the eyes of both of them were opened**, and they knew that they were naked; and they sewed fig leaves together and made themselves coverings.*

she think "why did she needed to be wise"?

The key question that struck Denise was this: When Scripture says that their "eyes were opened," *what eyes were opened?*

WHAT EYES WERE OPENED?

Obviously the physical eyes of the man and the woman in the garden were already open; they had been created with full physical aptitude. So when the Scripture says that their eyes were opened when they ate of the fruit of the tree it begs the question

- *What eyes were opened?*

It took the Lord quite a while to reveal the answer to that question. Sometimes the Lord waits to tell us the answers to our questions because we need to go through a process to bring us to a place where we can receive the answer that He wants to give us. That is the way it was with this question. When the Lord did answer, His answer came suddenly and unexpectedly as it often does. He said very clearly, *"The eyes that were opened were the eyes of the mind to understand the concept of good and evil."*

Those were the eyes that were opened! Until that time those eyes had not been opened. When the man and the woman ate of the fruit of the Tree of the Knowledge of Good and Evil they came into an entirely different type of seeing and a whole different kind of understanding. This different way of seeing and different mode of understanding had not been activated before but was now opened up to them when they partook of the fruit. Prior to that, they perceived with the eyes of the heart, eyes which saw love, acceptance, joy, and freedom. Those eyes now began to close and become inoperative. They no longer fellowshipped with the Father from their spirits and out of their hearts.

Once the eyes of the knowledge of good and evil are opened, the eyes of the heart begin to be blinded, the Tree of Life became blurred and the issues of good and evil, right and wrong, holy and unholy come into sharp focus. As we know from the passage in Genesis, the man and the woman were expelled from the garden because, from that point on, there was no way that they could commune and have fellowship with the Father. Satan had succeeded in luring them away from the simplicity of relationship with God into the complexities of the mind's ability to work out rights and wrongs, what is good and what is evil, holiness and unholiness.

When we look at Paul's preaching in the New Covenant we see that it is focused on reversing this action. In Ephesians 1:18, Paul prays that the "eyes of the heart" would be opened or 'enlightened.' He prays that the heart which had been shut down through the knowledge of good and evil might be enlightened and able to see again. Paul connects this in praying for the spirit of wisdom and revelation to be able to intimately know God. Wisdom and revelation come from the Tree of Life. When the eyes of the heart are opened they are open to wisdom and revelation. God can only be known through the wisdom and revelation which comes from Him.

Let me emphasise this point for it is crucial. When the eyes of the man and his wife were opened in the garden, the eyes that could partake, as it were, from the Tree of Life became dull. The eyes of the heart became blinded. Our original ancestors were expelled from the garden so that the Tree of Life was no longer accessible to them. God wanted to protect them from the unimaginable horror of being able to eat from *both* trees that were in the midst of the garden. Otherwise, by eating from the Tree of Life they would not have died, but would be forever trapped into eating from the Tree of the Knowledge of Good and Evil. Consequently, as a human race, we were left with only eating from the Tree of the Knowledge of Good and Evil.

LOSING UNION WITH GOD

When the man and his wife ate from the Tree of the Knowledge of Good and Evil a huge change happened in them. The moment their eyes were opened they became self-aware in their nakedness and sewed fig leaves together to cover themselves. They already knew that they were naked but it wasn't actually a problem for them until they ate of the tree. It had never occurred to them that there could be anything wrong with them. Yet when they ate from the tree, suddenly something was wrong! Their first thought was that they were flawed in some way, that something wasn't right with them. They were immediately aware of rights and wrongs, an awareness they had not had before! They take instant action to try to correct it by covering themselves. Making a wrong thing right was also a completely new idea for them.

As I was thinking about this one day a picture formulated in my imagination to help explain what happened to the man and the woman in the garden. I am going to have to ask you to exercise your imagination and follow my train of thought to get the point of this.

Imagine, for the purposes of my illustration, that the man and women in the garden (prior to eating of the tree) were physically green. I am borrowing a bit here from C. S. Lewis's *Perelandra*, in which he develops a character called 'the Green Lady' - at least I have Lewis's authority for my little imaginary scenario! *Perelandra* is an allegorical story, which alludes to the state of Adam and Eve in the Garden of Eden before the Fall. The woman in Lewis's story, whom he calls 'the Green Lady,' can be seen as a type of Eve before she partook of the fruit of the Tree of Knowledge.

Imagine then, that Adam and Eve, in the garden, were green; their skin tone was green. Now the colour green is made up of two other colours - blue and yellow. If you mix blue and yellow paint you will get green paint. If you imagine that yellow is representative of the earth and that blue represents heaven, Adam and Eve were a mix of heaven and earth. The combination of 'heavenly blue' of the Person of God and the 'yellow' clay of their humanity resulted in the greenness of a human life filled with God. That was God's intention for them. God poured His image into the clay and the two mixed together. Adam and Eve were created from the dust of the earth but they were totally in union with God Himself.

However, the moment that they eat from the Tree of the Knowledge of Good and Evil the union of their hearts with God is broken because they know that they have done what He told them not to do. From their standpoint, not God's, there is now a separation. Imagine that the 'blue' of God's nature was withdrawn and began to quickly fade away. They are now changing from 'green' to 'yellow' – back to the nature of humanness without the infilling of the personality of God. They realise with horror that they are naked and run to cover themselves with fig leaves.

Fig leaves are green. In covering themselves with fig leaves they are trying to make themselves what they had previously been. When they had union with God and everything was good they were 'green'; thus the fig leaves are an attempt to restore that 'greenness' to themselves. I believe that this has marked humanity throughout the millennia of human history. People have tried to put fig leaves on, covering themselves with earthly and worldly things, to cover up the fact that they are naked and without God. They are trying to make themselves acceptable again.

Nothing but the nature of God Himself can make us 'green' through and through. The fig leaves only give a surface appearance of green. Take them away and the fallen humanity

God in us, the hope of glory!

is obvious. Adam and Eve have a moment when they have gone against the God who loves them - and they know it. They did the very thing He expressly forbade them to do and suddenly something is wrong. They have just eaten from the knowledge of what is correct and incorrect. They are consumed with what is acceptable or unacceptable. The eyes of the heart are closed and these other eyes are opened. The eyes that could perceive love and acceptance are closing and the eyes of the mind are opened. The mind is useful in its own place - but it cannot see God. Your mind can only work out a way of doing what is right or wrong. It can only try to find fig leaves. It cannot relate in love and enjoy intimacy.

THE BASIS OF LEGALISM

It was a shock to us to realise that the problem is not just the knowledge of evil. That would seem to be obvious. The forbidden tree is *also* the tree of the knowledge of *good*. This is an entirely different matter. In fact, it becomes dangerous, because the question arises: how do we actually know what tree we are living from? It is not merely a matter of good versus evil and the correct option is to choose the good. No! The tree that was forbidden was the tree of the knowledge of both *good* as well as evil. It sounds so right that we should focus on discerning and doing what is good, as well as discerning and refraining from doing what is evil. But the truth is that the *whole operation* of discerning what is good and what is evil is feeding from the wrong tree and using the eyes that opened to Satan's tree.

How do we differentiate whether or not we are living out of the Tree of the Knowledge of Good and Evil or whether we are living out of the Tree of Life? You see, the Tree of Knowledge produces fruits that we believe are good. It is not all blatantly evil. That's the deceptiveness of it. All trees bear fruit and there are certain fruits that come from these two trees. By knowing what the fruits are you can tell what tree you are living from. So what are the fruits of the two trees? Let me look at the Tree of the Knowledge of Good and Evil first.

Living out of the knowledge of good and evil is the basis of legalism. It is where we decide for ourselves. It is where we choose based on our own values, seek to determine what is right and what is wrong, what is good and what is bad. It is the human mind constantly evaluating everything on the basis of one question – is it right or is it wrong?

We become 'the good and bad police' saying things like, "I'm good in such and such an area but bad in this other area." Self-condemnation and self-justification are to the fore. The fruit of this tree is that we make judgements on people – this person here is good but that person over there is bad. We bind ourselves in a constant dilemma of trying to work out the moral value of every action. We look at one another, judging one another's actions and words to see if they are good or bad. In doing this, we are living from the Tree of the Knowledge of Good and Evil.

I believe that the purpose of the Father's love is to take us away from that tree. His love fills us and frees us from having to live by this constant evaluation process. The constant evaluation of what is right or wrong means that we are caught in a snare and results in what Paul calls in Galatians 1:7 "no gospel at all" (NIV). You could paraphrase Paul's words to the Galatians like this:

"How did you ever think that this would work? God has given us His Spirit to live out of - and now, having come into the freedom and liberty of the Spirit, you are turning around and reverting to living by the Law. Law is always about rights and wrongs, about good and evil. You started in the Spirit and now you are trying to finish off in the flesh!"

The flesh loves this stuff! The flesh loves the Law! The flesh delights in the knowledge of good and evil. The flesh finds freedom very difficult. Living out of the Tree of the Knowledge of Good and Evil is to be bound in legalism. It is the basis of fear, the basis of all the striving that we get into, wondering if we have done enough. How do we even know whether or not we have done enough anyway? The fear of failure comes out of the Tree of the Knowledge of Good and Evil. We fear that we are inadequate. We fear that we haven't done well enough, that we are somehow not up to standard. We fear that we haven't succeeded. We judge ourselves and measure ourselves according to the benchmark of the Law to determine whether we are succeeding or failing. Even in our everyday lives we are affected by this. One example is the workplace, where we are constantly monitored on whether we are doing well enough. Much of our ambition and striving comes out of this. We are driven to be 'good enough,' to be 'right,' to be 'excellent'.

WHERE DOES THE TREE OF KNOWLEDGE ORIGINATE?

It is crucial to know where the Tree of the Knowledge of Good and Evil has originated. Contrary to what some might think, the Tree of the Knowledge of Good and Evil and the Tree of Life *did not* have their beginnings in the Garden of Eden. Genesis does not say that God *planted* these two trees in the Garden. Genesis 2:8&9 seems to indicate that the two trees were not planted by God in the same way as the other trees in the Garden:

> *The Lord God planted a garden eastward in Eden, and there He put the man whom He had formed. And out of the ground the Lord God made every tree grow that is pleasant to the sight and good for food. The Tree of Life was also in the midst of the garden, and the Tree of the Knowledge of Good and Evil.*

interesting supposition —

They had their origins somewhere else, before the creation of the world and the creation of man. The Tree of Life has its origins in eternity. It is a manifestation of all that God Himself is in His eternal nature. Its taproot is in the Godhead itself. The eternal nature of the Tree of Life is confirmed in Revelation 22. But where did the Tree of the Knowledge of Good and Evil originate? To gain insight into this we must turn to the prophet Ezekiel. In Ezekiel 28:12-15 we read:

> *"You were the seal of perfection,*
> *Full of wisdom and perfect in beauty.*
> *You were in Eden, the garden of God;*
> *Every precious stone was your covering:*
> *The sardius, topaz, and diamond,*
> *Beryl, onyx, and jasper,*
> *Sapphire, turquoise, and emerald with gold.*
> *The workmanship of your timbrels and pipes*
> *Was prepared for you on the day you were created.*
> *"You were the anointed cherub who covers;*
> *I established you;*
> *You were on the holy mountain of God;*

You walked back and forth in the midst of fiery stones.
You were perfect in your ways from the day you were created,
Till iniquity was found in you."

Then, in verse 17 we read:

"Your heart was lifted up because of your beauty;
You corrupted your wisdom for the sake of your splendor."

This passage is a prophetic declaration to the king of Tyre but it also speaks at a deeper level of Satan. It shows the origins of Satan who was once known as Lucifer, one of the archangels. I find it very interesting that Scripture tells us Satan has a heart. His heart was lifted up because of his extraordinary beauty. What I want to point out here, however, is that Satan had been full of the wisdom of God but his wisdom became *corrupted*. Until this time Satan had perfect wisdom, the same type of wisdom that was in God. He was filled with the wisdom of God but, because of his beauty, his heart was lifted up. He became arrogant and proud, desiring to displace God Himself and his wisdom became corrupted. What was the corrupted wisdom?

The corrupted wisdom was this. It came down to actions. It *had* been a wisdom that came out of the intimacy of love with Him who sees and knows all, but it became a wisdom founded in the ability to judge good and evil. It boiled down to doing what is right and not doing what is wrong. This was the corruption that happened and from then onwards this was Satan's wisdom. The Tree of the Knowledge of Good and Evil is more than just a tree. It is the manifestation of Satan's nature. It is the essence of his corrupted wisdom.

The knowledge of good and evil places a strong emphasis on right action as opposed to right motive. It ignores having the right heart. If the outward is good, then everything is OK. In contrast to this, Jesus emphasised the importance of having a right heart. His harshest criticism came to those who lived only to 'do the right thing.' "Whitewashed tombs," He called them. They were living out of the Tree of the Knowledge of Good and Evil. They may have acted well from an outward perspective, they may have excelled in 'doing the right thing' but their hearts weren't changed. You see, if the heart is right, even if the action is wrong or if the words don't come out as they should, people can receive it because they know that the heart is motivated by love. When you live by the knowledge of good and evil everything has to be perfect. So if you say or do the wrong thing then it is very wrong.

The Tree of the Knowledge of Good and Evil is the basis for performance-orientation and performance anxiety. Living out of that, if I'm not perfect then I'm not OK. Our worth is directly tied to our performance. We judge ourselves harshly, and by the same measuring stick we judge others harshly. You cannot judge yourself harshly without judging the other harshly and vice versa. Many religious groups exact these standards - if you are not measuring up to the standard then you are wrong and we cannot have fellowship with you. It is true on an individual and at a corporate level.

The law of sowing and reaping comes into play here. That is why Jesus said, *"Judge not, that you be not judged. For with what judgement you judge, you will be judged; and with the measure you use, it will be measured back to you."* (Matthew 7:1,2) Once we begin judging others on the basis of good and bad, right and wrong we open ourselves to be judged by the same standards.

This is a universal principle. Paul the apostle knew this when he said (1 Cor 4:3), "...in fact, I do not even judge myself." That is an astounding statement. Paul the apostle didn't make any judgements on himself! We are so conditioned to live our lives making constant judgements on the rightness or wrongness of our actions. We not only assess ourselves but others under the same spotlight. The apostle Paul refused to live out of the tree that judges right and wrong. We too need to do the same.

Much of this judging can be seen in popular Christian teaching. A lot of the teaching on discipleship emphasises the need for constant self-evaluation. Sad to say, much of this teaching is based on legalism, either blatant or subtle – but it is still legalism because it is from the Tree of the Knowledge of Good and Evil. It is not based on the gospel of the New Covenant that Jesus died to bring us into.

THE LAW OF SOWING AND REAPING

When we look at each other and evaluate each other, there are a whole set of spiritual laws that come into play. Principles such as the law of sowing and reaping. You sow a little seed of judgement but you reap in return a harvest of judgement. God intended the law of sowing and reaping to be something that would truly bless us. His desire was for us to reap an abundant harvest from one tiny seed. What a blessing that would be! To plant a few seeds and then, after a while, gain a whole field full of what you had planted in seed form. What is true in the natural realm is equally true in the spiritual realm. That selfsame principle originally designed to work in our favour can now work against us. We can sow a seed of discord or judgement and then, down the line, we begin to reap back what we have sown. We reap in the measure (or more) that we have sown in.

This is evident when we raise children. Oftentimes we swear to ourselves that we will *never* behave in the same way as our parents. We are determined to do things differently from our parents. But then something happens and we are shocked to hear the very words that our parents used come out of our own mouths. We have made judgements on our parents and now we are reaping the harvest of that judgement because we are treating our children in the same way. What we judge our parents for, we begin to act out in our own lives.

Another example comes to mind. Sometimes we find it incredulous that a woman who had an abusive father marries a husband who is very similar. Wouldn't she look for someone who is kind to her, who is loving and generous? Often, however, there is a judgement behind this. Scripture is very clear about this. The writer to the Hebrews explicitly warns, "...looking carefully lest anyone fall short of the grace of God; lest any root of bitterness springing up cause trouble, and by this many become defiled." (Heb 12:15) That root of bitterness can stay in the ground for many years, but once it comes to full maturity you reap it. It will come back to you many times over and in many different situations. A woman will grow up to marry a man just like the father she judged. A son will treat his child in the same way as the father that he judged. When you judge someone out of bitterness that selfsame judgement will come back on you.

Take yet another example. Why is it that a church that splits from another very often fails to thrive? Because it has been formed out of a judgement, and before long that same root manifests itself. Unless that bitter judgement has been dealt with and reconciliation occurs allowing love to flow again, the same judgement will manifest in the very next thing that you do! This is not something to be trifled with. It is an irreversible spiritual law.

Often people judge others for committing adultery. Then they succumb to the very same temptation themselves. Many of the problems in our lives stem from our own judgements; we become what we have judged. The truth is that judging others is nothing less than self-righteousness. Sometimes we take pride in the fact that we are standing up for righteousness. In reality, however, we have made judgements in our hearts. We do not see the plank in our own eye when we are trying to remove the speck out of the other person's eye.

The very powerful dynamic at work here is that all issues of judgement of wrongdoing in ourselves or others is a religious form of living that comes from eating from the Tree of the Knowledge of Good and Evil. When we do that there are inevitable consequences that follow on from it. Galatians 3:10 states very clearly:

> For as many as are of the works of the law are under the curse; for it is written, "Cursed is everyone who does not continue in all things which are written in the book of the law, to do them."

Many of us wonder why the blessing of God is not in our lives the way that He promised. Maybe we need to take time and ask the Holy Spirit to show us if there are any judgements lurking, if there are ways in which we have judged others *and ourselves* in trying to live under the Law. When we live under this Law we are living under a curse, because the whole system has been cursed. It is impossible to thrive under that.

LIVING FROM THE HEART

In my life and ministry I now place a huge emphasis on the life of my heart. The centrality of the heart is of the utmost importance in the Christian life. It is not out of our natural minds that we perceive anything spiritually – it is from our spirits and our hearts. It goes without saying that our minds are good because they are created by God. God intended for us to use our minds. His purpose, however, is that our minds will be operative when connected to the Tree of Life. In contrast to God's design, the other way for our minds to be used is for them to be connected to the Tree of the Knowledge of Good and Evil. When this is the case we are constantly using our minds to make value judgements about what is right and wrong; we have a need to live by formula and principle. We want to live our lives by rules. It is easier to refer to a *manual of laws* in a given situation than to make a decision from the heart. To live by guidelines is not using the 'mind of the Spirit' (Rom 8:6 & 27) to discern what to do in a given situation. Trying to work things out in our minds will bring spiritual death. The discernment and the knowing that comes from a heart-connection with the Tree of Life is totally different from trying to work everything out in our natural minds.

Consider this! In Ephesians 4:17, Paul says very strongly:

> *So I tell you this, and insist on it in the Lord, that you must no longer live as the Gentiles do, in the futility of their thinking. They are darkened in their understanding and separated from the life of God because of the ignorance that is in them due to the hardening of their hearts.* (NIV)

There are not many things that Paul writes so strongly, *insisting* in the Lord, and perhaps we would expect that he is going to say something about sexual sin, for example. Instead, he *insists in the Lord* that they no longer live in the futility of their thinking. What is more, Paul equates this futility of thinking with being 'darkened in understanding' and with being hardened in their hearts. That is very serious.

We see here the connection between the mind and the heart. When we are trying to live out of the Tree of the Knowledge of Good and Evil it is, according to Paul, 'futile thinking.' In other words, we cannot think properly if we are separated from our hearts. If our hearts are hardened we are ignorant of how the mind of God works. We are ignorant of His thoughts and His assessments because of a hardened heart. God's thoughts and assessments flow from His heart of love.

This is something that we can so easily miss. We need to be feeding from life rather than trying to work everything out. We can be free of worrying whether things are up to standard. If we live from the heart, connected to the Tree of Life, there is no need to be concerned with those things. It would be a huge relief just to be free of the compulsion to judge, and to then come into the life that flows from the heart of God. That is the real Gospel - to be connected to the life! What a relief and a joy to be in a place of having an open heart, moving in and with the heart of love that is in God, free from having to be constantly on our toes, assessing numerous spiritual decisions and issues every minute.

THE TREE OF LIFE

Let me now talk about the Tree of Life. Ironically there seems to be more to say about the Tree of the Knowledge of Good and

Evil than the Tree of Life. That is because the Tree of Life is actually very simple. The Tree of Life is simply this - it is being connected to and living in the love of God, abiding in the love that the Father and the Son enjoy in the bond of the Holy Spirit. We can live in a continuous experiencing of being loved by the Father and His Son Jesus. The Holy Spirit pours this love upon us over and over as we believe (Rom 5:5).

And there is a fruit to this Tree of Life. Galatians 5:22 gives a description of it. It is love, joy, peace, patience, kindness, goodness, faithfulness, gentleness and self-control. Paul says, "...against such things there is no law." This is what the love of the Father produces automatically in our lives.

We see this again and more pointedly in 1 Corinthians 13. In the opening verses God says that, no matter how gifted we are, if we don't have this love we are nothing. It then describes what God's love poured into you will produce in you:

> Love suffers long and is kind; Love does not envy; love does not parade itself, is not puffed up; does not behave rudely; does not seek its own, is not provoked, thinks no evil; does not rejoice in iniquity, but rejoices in the truth; bears all things, believes all things, hopes all things, endures all things. Love never fails.

This is what your personality will automatically become as the love of our Father pours into you. When we live according to the Tree of the Knowledge of Good and Evil we will act out of our decisions and knowledge of rights and wrongs. When we walk in the continuous experiencing of the Father loving us, however, our hearts will be transformed to be hearts after God's own heart and we will be motivated as He is and feel as He feels. His love pouring in will then overflow with all its characteristics, which we call the fruit of the Spirit.

We see the contrast of the life that flows from the two trees again in James 3:13-18:

> *Who is wise and understanding among you? Let him show by good conduct that his works are done in the meekness of wisdom. But if you have bitter envy and self-seeking in your hearts, do not boast and lie against the truth. This wisdom does not descend from above, but is earthly, sensual, demonic. For where envy and self-seeking exist, confusion and every evil thing are there. But the wisdom that is from above is first pure, then peaceable, gentle, willing to yield, full of mercy and good fruits, without partiality and without hypocrisy. Now the fruit of righteousness is sown in peace by those who make peace.*

When our fellowship is with God we are eating from the Tree of Life. When we are eating from the Tree of Life and when the eyes of our hearts begin to open we will then walk and live in the wisdom and revelation that Paul talks about in Ephesians 1. That is where life is. Life is no longer about the decisions between good and evil or right and wrong. It is about living from this enormity of love. This is love, to live in intimacy with the Father in His Son. This is what Adam knew in the garden before the Fall. Adam knew that life-connection with the Father.

THE COVERING OF LOVE

We are coming back to that life. This is the love that covers everything. This reality is beautifully demonstrated in Luke 7, when Jesus visited the house of Simon the Pharisee. It is ironic that most contemporary Bible translations put a heading about 'a sinful woman' above this section.

What happened here was an amazing thing in the culture in which this is set. These men in the house of the Pharisee had it all together. In their minds they were on their way to the new kingdom of God that was to be set up on earth. They guarded the Law with their lives. Keeping the letter of the Law was by far the most important thing for them. Every jot and tittle of the Law consumed their daily lives.

interesting point!

How intimidating it would have been for this woman to enter a room filled with the top men of society. They would have all been there, dressed in their finery, and very complacent in their fulfilling of the requirements of the Law. They had organised a special dinner and invited this rabbi, Jesus, to dine with them. They saw themselves as insiders in the purposes of God. I find it very interesting that these men knew who this woman is. They knew that she was a prostitute. Sometimes I wonder how they knew what her profession was!

There is something about what the presence of Jesus is to people who are broken, degraded, unclean and who are considered unworthy. The last resort of those of us who have nothing left is to come to Jesus. The most wonderful thing is that Jesus meets us in our brokenness. The presence of the Lord is so available. His presence is so real, because He has a heart for us. And in the midst of this scenario, this woman, the ultimate outsider, enters.

The Pharisees gathered in Simon's house judge her as a sinful woman. That wasn't Jesus' heart towards her, however. She comes in all her brokenness, having run out of every other option. She has been degraded by every possible means. Finally, at the end of herself, she is ready to risk it all. She pours out her heart to Jesus, her tears washing His feet. She possesses nothing but is giving everything that she has left.

What the Pharisees see is a prostitute give her calling card to a man who calls Himself the Son of God. They sit there wondering what His response will be. Is He a morally pure man? Can He deal with this situation in the appropriate manner? The book of Proverbs tells us that a prostitute is known by her kisses, her hair and her perfume. This woman is bringing the lot. The perfume is possibly what she uses for her work. Her hair and her kisses are tools of her work. That is all she has to give and she gives it all. She gives herself, and what remains of her dignity and self-presentation – the tools of her trade. She lays it all at Jesus' feet.

We see in verse 39 a demonstration of living from the Tree of the Knowledge of Good and Evil:

> *Now when the Pharisee who had invited Him saw this, he spoke to himself, saying, "This Man, if He were a prophet, would know who and what manner of woman this is who is touching Him, for she is a sinner."*

The Pharisee's judgement was clearly a judgement based on what was right and wrong, but Jesus defied that. The beautiful thing about this is that Jesus *was indeed* a prophet and He knew *exactly* who she was. In verse 40 we read:

> *And Jesus answered and said to him, "Simon, I have something to say to you." So he said, "Teacher, say it."*

Simon's response is because he wants more information to make his judgement on. But Jesus goes on to tell a parable:

> *There was a certain creditor who had two debtors. One owed five hundred denarii, and the other fifty. And when they had nothing with which to repay, he freely forgave them both. Tell Me, therefore, which of them will love him more?" Simon answered and said, "I suppose the one whom he forgave more."*

> *And He said to him, "You have rightly judged." Then He turned to the woman and said to Simon, "Do you see this woman? I entered your house; you gave Me no water for My feet, but she has washed My feet with her tears and wiped them with the hair of her head. You gave Me no kiss, but this woman has not ceased to kiss My feet since the time I came in. You did not anoint My head with oil, but this woman has anointed My feet with fragrant oil. Therefore I say to you, her sins, which are many, are forgiven, for she loved much. But to whom little is forgiven, the same loves little.*

Note that Jesus turns to the woman but addresses Simon. I can imagine that Jesus is filled with love and compassion as He looks at her. He knew that this woman had come with all that she had. I wonder if she was there when Jesus gave the Sermon on the Mount. Maybe she saw something in His eyes or heard something in His voice, something that marked Him out as different from any other man she had encountered. Her hunger and need for His love found an echo and an answer in Him. She knew somehow that He could love her in a way that she longed for. He loved her with a father's love, restoring dignity to her person. He displayed a love that far surpassed the moral code of what was perceived to be right and wrong

LOVE NEVER FAILS

How did this poor woman know that it was all about love? How did she know that the Christian life was not really about right and wrong, good or bad, or having it all together and doing the right thing?

It is so simple. The Tree of Life is about love that covers all the things that we spend so long examining the moral value of. If you love you cannot go wrong. When we commune with the Father the eyes of our hearts are opened again. The eyes that were closed when mankind took of the Tree of the Knowledge of Good and Evil will be closed again and the eyes of our hearts will be opened again so that we can eat freely from the Tree of Life. If we eat from the love of the Father we will love with the love of the Father!

When we really begin to walk in love, there is so much that we don't have to work out. If your heart is to eat constantly from the Tree of Life and judge with the judgement that brings freedom and mercy, it is so much easier to love than to do anything else. It is when we don't love that we have to evaluate everything. When we love, we can release people because it is not up to us to make a judgement on them.

May God grant us the beautiful innocence that Jesus had. He

didn't judge. He was the only one who could make the accurate judgements but He didn't do it. If it wasn't His job to judge, it is certainly not ours. There is so much more joy and freedom when you don't have to work out how much a person is right or wrong. If you have to bring correction, bring correction that gives life and not death. Discipline in love and care for the person is the way that restores them to life. The Tree of Life looks upon the heart, not the actions.

The Tree of Life is a foundation of love and freedom. Any judgement from the perspective of the love of God and in the flow of life is a right judgement. In contrast to that, judging from the other tree brings bondage and death. This is what James exhorts in chapter 2:12-13:

> So speak and so do as those who will be judged by the law
> of liberty. For judgement is without mercy to the one who
> has shown no mercy. Mercy triumphs over judgement.

Freedom and mercy are massive factors in this. Mercy triumphs over judgement. Where mercy is extended instead of judgement the will of God has prevailed. Mercy is letting the guilty go free and wishing for the guilty to be blessed. God sees us in this way. He looks upon us with mercy instead of judging us. His love does not punish us and therefore we have nothing to fear. According to 1 John 4:18 (NIV):

> There is no fear in love. But perfect love drives out fear,
> because fear has to do with punishment.

When we know that there is no more punishment because mercy has triumphed over judgement, then we no longer fear.

There is no fear in this love that God has for us. Sin that has been repented of carries no further judgement:

> *Who shall bring a charge against God's elect? It is God who justifies.* - ROM 8:33

There may be consequences in life for committing a sin but when it has been repented of, from God's perspective, His mercy triumphs over judgement. Judgement is one of the most serious issues between us and God. How can we sit in judgement over one of His people whom He has justified? If God no longer has an issue with that person, how can we mere mortals say that they are not worthy of our fellowship?

We are all in a process of learning to see with the eyes of love. People may say that "love is blind" but it is only love that truly sees. This issue of judging right and wrong has affected us all tremendously. You will never get a positive self-image within the Tree of the Knowledge of Good and Evil. You will only get that from the Tree of Life - from seeing yourself as God really sees you. Many of our problems come from eating from the wrong source. When we begin to eat from the Tree of Life those problems are dealt with.

I feel that we are well qualified to know this because, for so long, Denise and I lived so faithfully out of the Tree of the Knowledge of Good and Evil. We had great vision and determination to serve the Lord because He had done so much in us. We landed with a thud in the middle of light and life and we were very enthusiastic about reaching everyone. We got involved in everything and gave away everything that we had three or four times over. We became experts at ministry. Our big question in response to every need was, "What would Jesus do?" If that is your question you will end up getting very busy indeed. We did and we suffered severe burnout and found that it was not a part of God's Christianity.

Let me say this very clearly. If you can grasp this it will set you free from an incredible amount of 'Churchianity.' It can set you free from the legalistic mindsets and expectations that you have of yourself as a Christian. I really believe that it can set you free to simply enjoy your Christian life and your relationship with God. The whole point of the Tree of the Knowledge of Good and Evil is to lure you away from a simple relationship with your Father into another way of living, into another gospel which is not good news at all. Satan has been very effective in leading us astray. True righteousness, however, is about right relationship to God, not about right behaviour in the world. The Tree of Life is a connection of love with our Father. The one thing that never fails is love. If you eat from the Tree of Life you will naturally have grace for people and be able to forgive them. You will be patient and kind towards them and act correctly towards them. If your perspective is that you automatically see the things that are wrong in another person's life, then you are eating from the wrong tree. If your natural default is to see things wrong in your own life then you are eating from the wrong tree. The only Christian life that actually works is the one that flows from the Tree of Life.

CHAPTER TWO

~

Opening the Eyes of the Heart

The years of burnout that Denise and I went through had an incredible effect on us and we emerged from that time realising that something was very wrong with what we perceived Christianity to be. Yet having spent time in many nations and having seen Christianity in many different cultures, it seems that the predominant style of so-called Spirit-filled Christianity today is exactly what burned us out. In contemporary Christianity we are being greatly influenced by the way that the world operates. We are applying the same principles that operate in the business world to our walk with the Lord. To build a successful business you must be driven, structured, energetic and committed, so also to evangelise the world you must be a highly driven and goal-oriented person. The core principles of entrepreneurship involve having a dream, planning your dream, and then working your plan. If you work your plan diligently enough you *must* succeed. The same motivational techniques are applied in contemporary Christianity. There are motivational speakers who use exactly the same principles and turn spiritual life into a business project. There are even Christian preachers who can address the business world as motivational speakers because they promote the exact same principles to gain success. On the flip side of this, some churches are inviting the motivational speakers of the world to come and have input to the discipleship of their congregations. Church leadership meetings are often focused on zeal, commitment, planning, and keys to success. The concepts and values of the world are infiltrating the Church.

There has been a huge corruption of Christianity in these areas. I am becoming emboldened to speak more strongly than ever about these things, because I am seeing more and more clearly that once you start to plan the work of God in your spiritual life you have left the Holy Spirit out! You cannot plan the Holy Spirit; He will not fit into any plan. We may sing the words, "Not by might, nor by power but by My Spirit, says the Lord," with great gusto but then we go out and use all of our might and power to do the work of God. One of the great misconceptions in the Church is that Christianity can be understood through study alone, that it can be grasped in the human mind, and that you walk with God through your own efforts of self-control and discipline. We fail to realise that the Lord is not known or served through these methods. He looks upon the heart. God is looking for a heart relationship with us and His desire is that we would live from our hearts, not from what we think a Christian is *supposed* to do. Many think that we relate to God from our hearts but we work for Him with our efforts. We have lost sight of what Paul meant when he said that God worked within him mightily (Col 1:29) and Jesus said that the works that He did were not His works but it was the Father working in Him (John 14:10).

Before Adam and Eve ate from the Tree of the Knowledge of Good and Evil they had viewed life with different eyes. They had seen everything with the eyes of the heart. With those eyes they saw the love of God the Father for them and they saw themselves in the light of that love. Their relationship with each other was lived through the seeing of their hearts. The eyes of their hearts were operative and the eyes of the mind that evaluated right and wrong, good and bad, correct and incorrect were not operative. They were blind to those concepts and judgements. When they ate from the Tree of the Knowledge of Good and Evil they came into the same kind of knowledge that Satan operates from. Satan's nature is the judgement of good and evil. That is Satan's reality. He sees everything in the paradigm of good and bad. He is the original and ultimate legalist.

The serpent said, in effect, "God is doing a *bad* thing to you. He is withholding something *good*. He knows if you eat this fruit you will be like Him. He is trying to keep you in something negative. He doesn't want to give you the good stuff!" This was Satan's temptation. Once Adam and Eve ate from the tree their perspective of life began to become like Satan's. The eyes with which the serpent was seeing were opened for humanity. Prior to that their only concept was of God's love for them. They knew that they were forbidden to eat from the Tree of the Knowledge of Good and Evil but that was the only prohibition upon them. For them, everything was complete peace and joy. If you had sat down with them and attempted to explain the concept of insecurity, you could try for one hundred years but they would not have grasped it. Their whole experience was that Almighty God walked with them every day and completely and absolutely loved them. They were filled with that love so there was no capacity for fear or insecurity. What happened to them when they partook of the fruit was that their eyes were opened to be able to conceive of the possibilities of doing right or wrong, choosing good or evil. From that time onwards, the human race has been obsessed with that very issue and issues such as insecurity, fear and a negative self-image have become the norm.

Have you ever considered what it would be like to be physically blind? I have thought about it quite a bit. I am a very visual person and I just can't imagine what it would be like for people who cannot see. I have known some people who have lost their sight and it is a massive shock for them. So many of our sayings are connected to the concept of seeing. When we say goodbye we often say, "See you later," but that is never a real experience for the person who is blind. When you are blind you cannot see. When the eyes of the mind were opened the eyes of the heart were closed. The eyes that could see the reality of intimacy with the Father and His love for them closed, and as they went out of the garden the memory of walking with the Father began to fade. Over the next few generations that memory was lost to the world. They had heard about this God but no one could see Him. No one understood Him or knew who He truly was.

God then began to make overtures to the human race. He sent prophets, teachers, lawgivers and judges. He sent kings and poets, warriors and mothers of Israel. He sent them to somehow represent Him to a people who did not know Him and who could not see Him. The whole world was firmly entrenched in the paradigm that life was about right and wrong. It still is today. Even the tiniest details of our lives are seen in terms of right and wrong. "That's not the right colour of shirt to go with that jacket," or, "That is not the right way to style your hair."

From my reading of the Bible something has become increasingly clear to me. Since the Fall took place, God's agenda for the human race is that the eyes of the heart would be opened once more. Throughout the whole of the Scriptures we see time and time again that the issue of ministry has been about opening blind eyes to see the reality of who God is. To demonstrate this point, I want to pick out instances at different points in the history of God's dealings with humanity. These examples set out the mandate given by God throughout both the Old and the New Testaments.

THE MINISTRY OF MOSES THE LAWGIVER

In Deuteronomy 29 (starting at the beginning of the chapter), we read the story of the children of Israel coming out of Egypt and how the Lord did such great miracles for them. Moses reminds them of what the Lord did for them, parting the Red Sea, leading them through the wilderness, and giving them a land to possess:

Now Moses called all Israel and said to them: "You have seen all that the Lord did before your eyes in the land of Egypt, to Pharaoh and to all his servants and to all his land — the great trials which your eyes have seen, the signs, and those great wonders.

In verse 4, Moses then says these words:

...yet the Lord has not given you a heart to perceive, eyes to see, and ears to hear, to this very day...that you might know that I am the Lord your God.

In the midst of all the signs and wonders they had witnessed, they still had "no heart to perceive, eyes to see, and ears to hear."

What this is talking about is their inability to see with the eyes of the heart, to truly perceive and understand. The eyes of the heart of the people had been closed. Moses was able to see because his heart was different. His heart was not hardened, nor the eyes of his heart blinded. This is a very important juncture in the development of Israel. We see from this passage that the Israelites in general didn't have the capacity to see with the eyes that had been closed. They were seeing with the natural eyes, judging right and wrong.

THE MANDATE OF ISAIAH THE PROPHET

If we look at Isaiah, chapter 6, the same issue is raised. Isaiah was probably one of the greatest of the prophets. Large parts of his prophecy are in poetic form, although this is not immediately apparent when we read it in English. The book of Isaiah is an extraordinary book, not just because of what it says, but also because of how it says it. Isaiah was called to be a prophet. In the sixth chapter we read of a remarkable experience that he had:

> *In the year that King Uzziah died, I saw the Lord sitting on a throne, high and lifted up, and the train of His robe filled the temple. Above it stood seraphim; each one had six wings: with two he covered his face, with two he covered his feet, and with two he flew. And one cried to another and said:*
>
> *"Holy, holy, holy is the Lord of hosts;*
> *The whole earth is full of His glory!"*
> *And the posts of the door were shaken by the voice of him who cried out, and the house was filled with smoke.*
> *So I said:*

"Woe is me, for I am undone!
Because I am a man of unclean lips,
And I dwell in the midst of a people of unclean lips;
For my eyes have seen the King,
The Lord of hosts."
Then one of the seraphim flew to me, having in his hand a
live coal which he had taken with the tongs from the altar.
And he touched my mouth with it, and said:
"Behold, this has touched your lips;
Your iniquity is taken away,
And your sin purged."
Also I heard the voice of the Lord, saying:
"Whom shall I send,
And who will go for Us?"
Then I said, "Here am I! Send me."
And He said, "Go, and tell this people:
'Keep on hearing, but do not understand;
Keep on seeing, but do not perceive.'
"Make the heart of this people dull,
And their ears heavy,
And shut their eyes;
Lest they see with their eyes,
And hear with their ears,
And understand with their heart,
And return and be healed..."

When the prophet had this experience of seeing the Lord, he was undone. It wasn't that he was merely affected by the seriousness of the moment. He was flat on the floor, every atom of his body virtually falling apart. He was completely blown away and filled with a sense of his own profound nothingness. This has to be the ultimate emotional rollercoaster, from seeing the glory of God surrounded by seraphim to the deep realisation of his own uncleanness. He has seen God's glory *and* gone down to the depths. Now he is shot up to the heights as the angel touches his lips with the burning coal. He knows that his iniquity is taken away and his lips are cleansed. Now he can truly speak as a prophet.

Immediately the angel touches his lips, Isaiah hears the Lord asking this question, "Whom shall I send and who will go for Us?" God is waiting for Isaiah to volunteer. The Lord really wants us to be involved in what He is doing but He never coerces us to do anything. It is always our choice. He leads us - He doesn't drive us. If you are ever being driven by someone telling you that you *must* do something, you can know for sure that it is not from God. God will always draw you. Jesus said, "My sheep hear My voice and they follow Me." If you are not following by your free choice then it is not the Lord who is asking you to go that way.

Here we have this incredible scenario in which the Lord touches Isaiah and then the prophet hears the Godhead begin to converse with one another. He heard the voice of the Lord saying, "Whom shall I send and who will go for Us?" Imagine that all this is happening to Isaiah at one level - witnessing the glory of God filling the temple, seeing the angels round the throne, having his lips touched by a burning coal from the altar. And the Godhead - Father, Son and Holy Spirit - are letting Isaiah overhear their conversation. The Persons of the Godhead allow this man to hear what they are saying to one another. I find it amusing to imagine their discussion like this:

> *"Who shall we send? Have you got any ideas?"*
> *"I wonder..."*

Then Isaiah, almost reluctantly, speaks up and says these amazing words, *"Here am I."*

"Oh yes, so you are!" God is apparently leaving it up to Isaiah to volunteer. And he then responds,

"Here am I, send me. I will go and speak Your word."

Now here is the important part. This incredible experience that God granted to Isaiah was to headline the commission that He was about to give to him. The Lord then speaks directly to Isaiah and what He tells him to say becomes the basis for the prophet's whole life and ministry:

> *"Keep on hearing, but do not understand;*
> *Keep on seeing, but do not perceive.*
> *Make the heart of this people dull,*
> *And their ears heavy,*
> *And shut their eyes;*
> *Lest they see with their eyes,*
> *And hear with their ears,*
> *And understand with their heart,*
> *And return and be healed."*

What God is saying here is: "I am sending you to preach My word but when you do that, they are not going to receive it. They have already made up their minds to My word being all about rights and wrongs, but I am sending you anyway as a witness. I am sending you off in a ministry to a people who are not going to listen. In fact, your preaching will close up their ears *even more*."

Some ministry commission this is! The ministry of the prophet will bear *no* fruit. Quite the opposite – it will drive people further away. This really challenges our idea of what ministry truly is.

God is sending the prophet to preach this word but at the same time He tells Isaiah that the people will not listen. They will not have eyes to see or ears to hear. They will not have the capacity to understand. Why? Because their hearts are hardened and they are locked into using their other eyes – *the eyes that judge what is right and wrong.* They are heading down the path of being obedient to law. They already have great knowledge in their heads, so as Isaiah preaches from his heart to theirs there will be no response. The word of God always appeals to the heart and the hardened heart can never receive it.

We are locked into the same issue – the issue of right and wrong. We can be so sin-focused. Do you know that God has no interest whatsoever in sin? His only occupation with sin is to get rid of it. He is not morbidly interested in the details of sins – evaluating good ones and bad ones. He just wants to get rid of the lot. He is not thinking, "Oh, you terrible, terrible person – you're a sinner!" Of course He knows that you are a sinner! You were born in Adam. There is no hope for you, except in Jesus. Jesus has washed away our sins. How many of our sins has Jesus washed away? All of them! It is not about sin. It is not about right and wrong! It is about having your eyes opened to something else. It is about seeing another reality.

Even as Christians our eyes are opened to right and wrong. Our value system is based on sin and the righteousness of actions. Our eyes are open to doing what is good and refraining from doing wrong. It is all about the *shoulds* and the *should nots*. The reality is about something different. When you are looking at right and wrong, holiness or evil, you are still living your Christian life out of the wrong tree - the Tree of the Knowledge of Good and Evil. That phrase "the wrong tree" has brought such clarity to us. Now Denise and I often look at each other when we react in a certain way to a circumstance and say, "Wrong tree!"

Here is an interesting question to ponder. Do you think that God wakes up every morning and thinks, "I must not sin today"? Of course not! He *naturally* doesn't sin. How does He do that? *Because He lives by a different principle of life.* He lives by the law of love - *and love cannot sin.* The love of God cannot commit any sin. Even if a heart of love doesn't really understand what sin is, it still won't sin - because love cannot sin. Love only wants the best and does the best for the one that it loves. Love cannot steal from a person that it loves. Love cannot lie to the one whom it loves. When you love somebody you are not going to murder them. Love naturally and automatically fulfills the law. It is the eyes of the heart that focus on love but it is the eyes of the natural mind (the flesh) that see good and bad. The whole issue of Isaiah's life and ministry was exactly what God had said to him: these people are locked into seeing with the eyes of the knowledge of good and evil and they cannot be healed.

THE MINISTRY OF JESUS

Now let us jump forward to Jesus' day. In Matthew 13 from verse 13 onward we read of Jesus and how all of His preaching and teaching was also built around this very same issue of the eyes and ears of the heart being activated. He said:

> *Therefore I speak to them in parables, because seeing they do*
> *not see, and hearing they do not hear, nor do they understand.*
> *And in them the prophecy of Isaiah is fulfilled, which says:*

"Hearing you will hear and shall not understand,
And seeing you will see and not perceive;
For the hearts of this people have grown dull.
Their ears are hard of hearing,
And their eyes they have closed,
Lest they should see with their eyes and hear with their ears,
Lest they should understand with their hearts and turn,
So that I should heal them."

But blessed are your eyes for they see, and your ears for
they hear; for assuredly, I say to you that many prophets
and righteous men desired to see what you see, and did not
see it, and to hear what you hear, and did not hear it.

The reality is this. We are living in the same day as Isaiah and in the same day as Jesus. The hearts of the people are *still* dull. They are dull because the eyes of the heart have become closed, and the eyes of the knowledge of right and wrong, correct and incorrect are open.

The fruit and strength of the wrong tree is not that it consists in the knowledge of evil. The insidious power of the wrong tree is that it is the knowledge of *good* as well as evil! *We are deceived because we believe that the knowledge of 'good' is a godly thing.* How can you argue against doing good? Let me state this clearly; because something is 'good' it is not necessarily God! God is not about choosing the 'good'. God's nature is love and that is what He is about. He is looking for love not what is good!

As soon as you ask the question, "What does the Bible say about this?" or "What is the right thing to do?" or even "What would Jesus do?" - you are in the wrong tree. If the question is in the wrong tree then the answer will most certainly be in the wrong tree. Someone said to me once about a sin issue that had arisen within church leadership, "This has nothing to do with love. It's about truth!" That seemed absurd to me. How can anything Christian be nothing to do with love? *God* is love! Anything and everything in Christianity has to be based on the outworking of love. Love and truth are one!

Jesus told parables to try to open the eyes of people's hearts. The parables were not to be analysed by the mind – they could only be understood at a heart level. That was the whole point of Jesus' ministry – to get the ears of the heart to hear, the eyes of the heart to see, and the heart to understand. When Jesus spoke for the first time in the synagogue (Luke 4: 16-21), He read from the scroll of the prophet Isaiah: "The Spirit of the Lord is upon me because He has anointed me...to *give sight to the blind*." I do not believe that He is primarily talking in this instance about the physically blind. I believe that He is primarily talking about the eyes of the heart. His ministry, which He received from the Father, was to open the blind eyes of the heart.

Consider this; how did Jesus choose the twelve disciples? They were the rejects, so to speak, after the cream of Jewish religious society had been taken for training in the rabbinical schools. How did Jesus know to pick the twelve who were His closest followers? Jesus had the capacity, given by His Father, to be able to read hearts. He could see the ones that the Father had given to Him. They were the ones whose hearts were open to receive the love that the Father had for them. At the outset of His earthly ministry He is 'lumbered' (as some might think) with a motley bunch of men. There were some fishermen, a self-obsessed and wealth-focused tax collector, a Zealot (one who advocated the violent overthrow of the Romans) - they were the dregs, the riffraff of society.

I *love* the dregs. I love working with those who have been ignored and rejected. Generally speaking, people pick the really promising ones who look good on paper. I'm very happy with that because it gets them out of the way. The way is now clear to see who the rejects are. Jesus chose those rejects who had the right heart and who proved it. Most of them ended their lives as martyrs. He passed on to the disciples the responsibility of the salvation of the human race. It was a huge responsibility. Jesus carried the responsibility of the salvation of the human race upon Himself and when He rose from the dead and went back to heaven, that responsibility was passed to the Twelve. If He had not trusted that they, in the power of the Spirit, could do this what hope would there be for any of us? But He had chosen men of good hearts, men whose 'heart-eyes' had been opened. They were not focused on right and wrong but became channels of the love of God.

We need to understand that the Gospel is about the love of God. It is not about righteousness. Love is always and without exception righteous. Righteousness is the product, not the core. The Church today struggles with love. It struggles with love between individuals, between leaders, between denominations. Many senior leaders cannot trust the young and upcoming leaders. The young and upcoming leaders have difficulty loving their elders. Why do we struggle with love? Because we haven't experienced it. Our eyes have been opened to right and wrong instead, and we have lived our Christian life based on that evaluation. All so-called 'Christian' conflicts are founded and energised by perspectives of right and wrong, good and evil.

Any resolution from within that perspective is weak and flawed because it is based in the mind which cannot love.

There is a much easier way: be filled with the love of the Father until that love becomes the expression of your life. When you are filled with the love of the Father you will discover an interesting thing. You will discover that you are not interested in sin anymore. Neither are you interested in trying to work out what is right and wrong. You just want to love - and you will discover that love cannot sin. The love of God cannot sin. Human love may sin but God's love cannot. God's love is His very nature. The only way that we can love with His love is to be full of it. If the eyes of your heart can become wide open, you will experience Him loving you in a way that you have never done before. His love for you will not change but your experience of it will because you will be able to receive it in your heart. God's love always and only comes to the heart.

PAUL'S MINISTRY COMMISSION

We see this divine mandate of opening blind eyes continued in the ministry of the apostle Paul. Paul is probably the most significant writer in the New Testament. I personally think that Paul, to some extent, may be more significant for us than the Twelve because (like us) he never saw Jesus face to face. He was not a disciple of Jesus in the literal and physical sense. Thus he came into Christianity like you or I would. Being struck blind on the road to Damascus is not what you may call normal but the truth is that Paul became a believer through an encounter with the risen Jesus. During that encounter Paul was given his ministry commission.

If we turn to Acts 26:12-18 we can see in more detail what transpired during the Damascus Road encounter. Here, Paul is testifying before King Agrippa:

> *While thus occupied, as I journeyed to Damascus with authority and commission from the chief priests, at midday, O king, along the road I saw a light from heaven, brighter than the sun, shining around me and those who journeyed with me. And when we all had fallen to the ground, I heard a voice speaking to me and saying in the Hebrew language, 'Saul, Saul, why are you persecuting Me? It is hard for you to kick against the goads.' So I said, 'Who are You, Lord?' And He said, 'I am Jesus, whom you are persecuting. But rise and stand on your feet; for I have appeared to you for this purpose, to make you a minister and a witness both of the things which you have seen and of the things which I will yet reveal to you. I will deliver you from the Jewish people, as well as from the Gentiles, to whom I now send you,* **to open their eyes, in order to turn them from darkness to light, and from the power of Satan to God,** *that they may receive forgiveness of sins and an inheritance among those who are sanctified by faith in Me.*

We see clearly here that Paul had the *same commission* as Moses, Isaiah and Jesus. His ministry would be a ministry of opening the eyes of the heart so that the people could perceive the real truth. This passage is saying that, if the eyes of the heart are not opened and if you are just living by the eyes of the mind, you are still walking in Satan's way. In other words, living by the eyes that see right and wrong is Satan's way of living.

Acts 28 states this again. Paul had been preaching to these

people from Moses and the Prophets (v.25) concerning Jesus. He had been speaking to them from morning till evening and they didn't like what Paul was saying:

> *So when they did not agree among themselves, they departed*
> *after Paul had said one word: "The Holy Spirit spoke*
> *rightly through Isaiah the prophet to our fathers, saying:*
>
> *'Go to this people and say:*
> *"Hearing you will hear, and shall not understand;*
> *And seeing you will see, and not perceive;*
> *For the hearts of this people have grown dull.*
> *Their ears are hard of hearing,*
> *And their eyes they have closed,*
> *Lest they should see with their eyes and hear with their ears,*
> *Lest they should understand with their hearts and turn,*
> *So that I should heal them."*

Paul quotes directly from the sixth chapter of Isaiah here. We see from this that Paul's preaching comes down to the very same issue. From Moses to Isaiah, from Isaiah to Jesus and then through to Paul - the issue of all ministry is about opening the eyes of the heart. It is not about teaching precepts and principles but its goal is to open the eyes that have been blinded - the eyes of the heart. Because when the eyes of the heart are opened you are turned away from the knowledge of good and evil to God Himself.

Remember where this knowledge of good and evil originates. It originates in Satan's corrupted wisdom, which aspired to *become like God*. I pointed this out in the previous chapter, quoting from Ezekiel 28. Satan operated out of his corrupted wisdom, which can be reduced to choosing what is right and refraining from what is wrong. That is why I have said, that as the Tree of Life is a manifestation of God's nature so the Tree of the Knowledge of Good and Evil is a manifestation of the nature of Satan.

Let me be clear here, in case of any misunderstanding. It is clearly wrong to do things such as exceeding the speed limit, or even murder. There is no question about that. When it comes to the practical issues of life we have to make choices often between right and wrong. Is it right or wrong to walk in front of a bus? Of course it is wrong! If you are a doctor or a nurse you need to know what is the right thing to do. I, for sure, want to be treated by doctors who know how to do the right thing medically. There are things that you clearly know are wrong to do. But when we are talking about *our relating to God and our walk with Him* - right and wrong have *nothing* to do with it. This is talking about your personal walk with God in intimacy and ministry flows out of that. You don't get peace by doing the right thing as a Christian. You get peace by forgetting about what is right and wrong and falling into His love. When you fall into His love you will get filled with it and you will be able to do nothing else but love - *and love cannot sin.*

The only way that we can love with God's love is to be full of His love. Jesus died on the cross so that we could come boldly to the throne of grace, jump on the lap of the Creator of the universe and find total acceptance in His arms. When Paul is talking about being delivered from the power of Satan to God, it is the same reality as being turned from darkness to light. To me that is quite important. When trying to live by the rights and wrongs one thing you will discover is this. The longer you live the longer the list of rights and wrongs gets. There is no end to it. It is a continuous source of condemnation. No matter how good you get there will be new things that pop up all the time that you didn't know about or that you haven't done yet. The major problem for Christians today is condemnation, a pervading sense of somehow not being up to scratch. We feel too condemned to seek God for the answers to our lives, so we flock to conferences to receive a personal prophecy. The reality is that no one is any closer to God than you are. He lives in your heart.

THE PURPOSE OF MINISTRY

This is what all ministry really boils down to. As I have shown from these passages of Scripture, the issue of ministry throughout all time since the Garden of Eden is that the eyes of our hearts will be enlightened. From God's perspective, the singular goal of the Gospel is that the eyes of the hearts of people will be opened so that He will be known. God's heart is that every minister of the Gospel would have as their mandate to open the eyes that have become blind - the eyes of the heart. As a preacher, I am keenly aware that this is the mandate given to me by God - to open blind eyes so that the eyes of the heart become operative. As your heart becomes alive understanding will come to you. I never realised that the place of receiving revelation is the place of love. Yet when you consider this it is so blatantly obvious. If you want to experience something from God the closer you are to love the more you are going to experience it. Why? Because God *is* love. When you are in harmony you have ears to hear from Him. He speaks from the heart and reveals Himself to the eyes of the heart. Understanding is far superior to knowledge. Knowledge is a byproduct of understanding and love brings understanding.

The more open your heart becomes, the more of God you will see, the more you will hear, and the more you will be healed.

We have spent many years praying for people to get healed and we have seen some incredible emotional healings take place. Now, I want to bring people into the flow where healing will continually happen. You can give a hungry man a fish or you can teach him how to fish. Which is best? I am less focused on praying for personal healing now because I want to tell people how to get into the stream of Father's love for them. Once a person's heart is open to *His love,* healing will continue throughout their whole life.

I do not want to put my hope in anything apart from my enjoyment of my walk with my Father. If you stop enjoying that intimate relationship your heart will begin to close again. Ambitions, dreams, productivity, goals and strategies will become your focus. Then the eyes of your heart will begin to close. As someone said, "I focused so strongly on my vision that I lost my sight." We can get a vision from God and focus so strongly on it that we lose the ability to see with spiritual eyes. Enjoy your personal walk with the Father. Enjoy His love for you. Revel in Him loving you. As you do, the eyes and ears of your heart will open wider. Your understanding and perspective of God in your life will grow. If you talk to others and He is loving on you while you are talking they will experience that love too. Open your heart to experience it while you are talking and the substance of that love will flow through you to those who are listening. We call it 'anointing' but it is just God being Himself through you.

I am writing this to give you hope. Don't be discouraged if you find this in you. It is normal for us to be seeing with the wrong eyes. It is normal for us to have the eyes of our hearts blinded and not functioning. I am bringing this out to demonstrate that the eyes that see right and wrong are actually not the valid eyes for

★ Good point.

Christianity. If we can understand that this is locking us into a wrong gospel then the eyes of the heart can become stronger and open up to see the truth.

You may be wondering whether the eyes of your heart are open. How do you know? All you need to do is ask yourself one question – Do you like what you are reading here? Do you resonate with what I am communicating to you? You see, if you like this, it is your heart that likes it. It is the eyes of your heart that are open to enjoy the truth of this. Don't worry about how *wide* your eyes are open. Just realise that God is opening them more and He will continue to do so. The more He opens the eyes of your heart the more you will be able to believe and receive the love of the Father for you. Conversely, when we tune in to what is right and wrong the love of the Father is blocked from our hearts. It is blocked because all you can see is your own unworthiness and what you must do to rectify it. The flow of love will be restricted. The truth is that God loves you because of *His* nature, not your merit. He loves you because He *is* love. He loves you because He created you. He cannot fail to love you. The only way into the eternal love of God is through Jesus but He loves you even if you haven't come yet. God so loved the world that He gave His Son for it.

This is a revelation that will totally captivate your heart, and in times of weakness you cannot deny the reality of what you have already seen. Your perspective of God is changed through revelation. You can deny what you have learned intellectually but you cannot deny what you have seen by revelation. Revelation is the opening of the eyes of the heart to see how God sees. Revelation enables people to see who God truly is and what it really means to walk with Him.

CHAPTER THREE

~

The Third Law

This first section of the book has so far explored the huge paradigm shifts that have taken place in our walk with God. The realisation that we have been living life out of the wrong tree and that the eyes of our hearts need to be opened to perceive the reality of who God is, becomes the true foundation for our Christianity. This revelation of the love of the Father is a new foundation in contrast to the old foundation of the knowledge of good and evil. In reality, however, it is only a new foundation because our eyes have been blinded. The Tree of Life is the true foundation of our walk with God. The opening of the eyes of the heart is the only way to know Him for He is only known by revelation. In this chapter I will write about another major paradigm shift that I saw recently.

WHAT THE GOSPEL REALLY IS

Since I have come into this revelation of the Father's love and begun to walk in sonship, I feel for the first time in my life that I understand what the Gospel actually is. Being a Christian for as long as I have you would think I would have an idea what it is but I really haven't, though I am beginning to see it now.

I wonder if much of professing Christianity truly understands what the Gospel is. The Body of Christ is full of very sincere people. We are blown away by meeting the many believers that we have fellowshipped with around the world. The lives that they have lived, what they are doing, and what is in their hearts. We are regularly floored in amazement at such people. We really love the Body of Christ. Yet in the midst of that I feel that many people are living the Christian life without any real grasp of what it actually is. Years ago Denise and I were speaking to a group of youth leaders in Fiji. We were speaking at a meeting in a thatched hut that had no walls. The roof was supported by wooden poles. As a speaker I can pick up whether or not people are getting what I am saying. I can see in their eyes whether or not I am getting through. As I was speaking I was astonished at how little my audience actually knew. Most of them couldn't read or write so I was trying to make my words as simple as possible. Most of them hadn't been exposed to the level of teaching that we have. I remember commenting to Denise how amazing it was that they were so zealous with so little understanding. At the time I wondered what they were so zealous about considering that they knew very little. Now I see that they were zealous because they had experienced the reality of God to them.

For the last twenty years I have felt like I have been standing in a river of revelation. I don't fully know where this is going or where it ends but it is wonderful and extraordinary. Some of this revelation is striking and contemporary Christianity will struggle with it. We have walked a solitary path because of this. When we receive revelation on something, so much else within Scripture is triggered off. It is like putting a piece into a jigsaw and suddenly you see where ten other pieces fit. That is a very exciting place, but it is also a lonely place.

This is very threatening to the "Status quo".

Sometimes you battle for years and years with something that you read in Scripture, struggling with a statement or a concept that you cannot really grasp. I had wrestled with a particular passage throughout my Christian life (and I have been a Christian for more than forty years) but just recently I saw what it meant. It didn't come to me in a flash of revelation as such. It was more like a dawning realisation of what the Gospel really is. When this understanding began to dawn on me it shook me considerably.

The passage I am referring to is Romans chapter 7. As I was reading Romans 7 and continued into chapter 8, I got a revelation as to what it was talking about, and I really felt like it was the closing of a circle in my walk with the Lord. I received an incredible level of understanding of something that was basic and foundational. I always take a risk when I share revelation because often people may not grasp what I am trying to convey. You cannot, however, force revelation upon people. People can only receive the next step. There are developments of understanding that need foundations of revelation laid over a long period of time, in order to be able to grasp a greater understanding. You are only able to hear or see what you are ready to hear or see. When this occurred to me I felt for the first time that I was beginning to understand where Paul was coming from. Personally speaking, I identify with others more than I do with Paul but in this area I feel that I am beginning to understand his perspective. Now that is exciting. So to begin, let me go back to the Old Testament to the prophet Ezekiel.

THE PROPHECY OF EZEKIEL

The book of Ezekiel contains a verse that began to turn my eyes in a different direction. The Old Testament prophets began to prophesy about the coming New Covenant that God would bring into the world. He had chosen a people descended from Abraham to be a witness to Him to all the nations of the world. This was to be a fulfillment of His promise to Abraham that all the nations of the world would be blessed through his offspring. The Law was given through Moses on Mount Sinai, but the Law could never be fulfilled. The Law is there to show you that you cannot possibly keep it! But the prophets prophesied a new day that would come and they were foreseeing the coming of Jesus. In this passage from Ezekiel (36:22-28) we have one of the major examples of the foretelling of this new day:

> *"Therefore say to the house of Israel, 'Thus says the Lord God: "I do not do this for your sake, O house of Israel, but for My holy name's sake, which you have profaned among the nations wherever you went. And I will sanctify My great name, which has been profaned among the nations, which you have profaned in their midst; and the nations shall know that I am the Lord," says the Lord God, "when I am hallowed in you before their eyes. For I will take you from among the nations, gather you out of all countries, and bring you into your own land. Then I will sprinkle clean water on you, and you shall be clean; I will cleanse you from all your filthiness and from all your idols. I will give you a new heart and put a new spirit within you; I will take the heart of stone out of your flesh and give you a heart of flesh. I will put My Spirit within you and cause you to walk in My statutes, and you will keep My judgements and do them. Then you shall dwell in the land that I gave to your fathers; you shall be My people, and I will be your God."*

Here again we can see the truth that, as Christians, we are to walk by love not by right and wrong and not by trying to judge our own rights and wrongs or those of other people. When the man and his wife saw the Tree of the Knowledge of Good and Evil they perceived that it was good for food. It *does* look like a very attractive way to live life. What is more, people who live from that tree look really good. We see these people as exemplary Christians, because we are evaluating on the basis that they do everything right. The fruit of the tree looks good for food, it looks attractive and those who eat of it look very attractive too. It appears as if it will make you wise. You will look like someone who knows all the right stuff. It really looks like I will become wise by walking down this path. The catch is, however, you are always limited by what *you* think is right, according to *your limited perspective* of what holiness means. It only goes as far as your education. Christianity, however, is measured by love.

In Ezekiel 36:26-27 we read a short description of what the New Covenant is going to do when God establishes it. This is where living in the love of God will take you. In contrast to the Old Covenant, this declares that God will establish a fresh and new covenant.

In verse 26 of chapter 36, we see a description of this new covenant. He says:

> *"I will give you a new heart and put a new spirit within you; I will take the heart of stone out of your flesh and give you a heart of flesh."*

You need to know that when the Bible uses the word 'new' it is often used interchangeably with the word 'renew.'[1]

---

1. *The Hebrew word used here is chadash or chadashah (feminine), which carries the meaning 'to renew' or to 'make fresh.'*

When God says, "I will give you a *new* heart and put a *new* spirit within you," He is making a *redemptive* statement. He is talking about a human spirit that is *renewed*. The 'heart of stone' is the same heart that is described in Jeremiah 17:9 as 'desperately sick.' When God gives you a new heart it is a good heart - no longer of stone but a heart of flesh. That is why when we are filled with the Spirit of God our heart will begin to desire the things of God. We can then be led by the Spirit of God - in our hearts. God will give us the desires of our hearts that we can then begin to walk in. He renews our hearts and renews our human spirits. Then He promises to put His Spirit within us. Here comes the word that had such an impact on me:

> "I will put My spirit in you and CAUSE you to walk in My statutes and keep My commandments."

When we live our Christian life out of the Tree of the Knowledge of Good and Evil, it is not actually Christian life. It is an Old Testament lifestyle of keeping laws but we are doing it *after* we are saved. I call it 'Old-Covenant Christianity.' Consequently we are robbed of the power of salvation and what the Gospel really is. In doing what is good and refraining from doing what is bad we are *causing ourselves* to do it. Either God causes us to walk in His ways or we cause ourselves - and only God can really cause us. His way in our Christian lives is that He is both "...the will and the do!" (Phil 2:13) There is really no alternative to keeping His commandments than Him causing us to do it. When we are independent of God the onus is *on us* to do it. You have to make the right decisions. Our Christian life has been motivated by our own ability to be decisive, to discipline and fashion our own actions.

The Lord's promise through Ezekiel is that *He would cause* us

- that is the essence of the New Covenant. He is saying, "I will change your motivation and I will cause you to do the things that I delight in." When I hear that promise all I can do in response is cry out, "Let me have it!" If God can change me so that, when I am faced with temptation, it will not be my effort or discipline that will resist the temptation. Rather, God is somehow going to *cause* me to do the right thing. He will cause me to do what He would do. I want that!

Years ago I said to the Lord, "Whatever it takes. I don't care how painful it is. Would You just cut out of me whatever it is that stops me from being like Jesus? Please do an instant 'Jesu-fication' on me. I don't care how much it hurts!" Well, nothing actually happened in response to that prayer, but I didn't understand this New Covenant reality that He would *cause* me to do what He would do. I didn't realise that this was the real promise of the Gospel - that God would do it all!

PAUL'S DISCOURSE IN ROMANS

This brings me to Romans 7, a chapter that I have really loved. The first four verses were clear to me. In these Paul explains how we got free of the obligation of the Old Covenant so that we can come into a New Covenant in our relationship with God. In God's sight the Old Covenant was like a marriage, and thus was unable to be dissolved. I know that divorce is prevalent today and marriage does not seem to have the same significance in our culture, but Paul's metaphor of marriage is intended to underline the permanence of the Old Covenant.

The covenant which God makes with Israel goes right back to Abraham. When God made this covenant with Israel as far as He was concerned it was a marriage covenant. It was a commitment that would last the lifetime of both parties. We see this reality throughout the Old Testament, particularly in the book of Hosea. God tells the prophet to marry a prostitute so that when she is unfaithful to Hosea (which she was), he will know how God feels when Israel is unfaithful to Him. God likens His relationship with His people to that of a marriage.

Paul says in Romans 7 that marriage is a binding covenant until one party dies. There is no way that the covenant can be broken until 'death do us part.' The covenant continues unbroken as long as there are Israelites. It was given to Abraham and his children's children. Paul says here, however, that the Old Testament covenant no longer has any hold over us. You may wonder how the covenant was broken. I can tell you how God got out of that covenant. *He died.* The covenant stands as long as both partners are alive, but when Jesus died on the cross the covenant was finished. *never thought of this before!*

The essence of the Old Covenant, in a nutshell, was this: "You do what I say, keep the Law of Moses and the Ten Commandments and I will bless you." This is why, when we live our Christianity out of the Tree of the Knowledge of Good and Evil, we are still living as if we are under the Old Covenant. We are still living in a conditional agreement. Blessing is only guaranteed if we do the right thing. I have observed that quotation from Joshua on the walls of many Christian homes, "Choose ye this day whom ye will serve. As for me and my house we will serve the Lord." In other words, "If you choose to do the right thing I will bless you." That mindset is the mindset of the Old Testament. That is *not* the New Covenant.

The essence of the New Covenant is this: I will put My Spirit in you and CAUSE you to walk in My ways. This is a direct contrast with the Old Covenant, which states: "These are My ways - do them!" The Old Covenant agreement puts the onus on *you* to do it! The opening verses of Romans 7 spell out that the Old Covenant is now over because Jesus died on the cross. When He died on the cross another extraordinary thing happened - *you* died as well! We *all* died with Him! In the same way, when He rose from the dead, the whole creation was affected because He holds all creation together by the substance of His being. (Col 1:17) All of creation holds together in Christ so when Jesus died on the cross, what happened to the substance that He holds together? It died. When He rose from the dead what happened? Everything rose with Him. *It's all new !*

THE OLD COVENANT IS FINISHED

My focus here, however, is this. When Jesus died, the Old Covenant marriage was over. It is interesting to see the magnitude of this reality even played out historically. Within a very short time after the death of Jesus, Jerusalem was ransacked by the Romans and the temple was razed to the ground. The Levitical priesthood ceased to function and the descendants of David could no longer be traced. That era, the Old Covenant era, was well and truly over. I do not intend to enter any debate about the Jewish people but I do know this, when they recognise Jesus as Messiah, salvation is as open to them as it is to us. Without Christ there is no hope for either Jew or Gentile. There is only salvation for all human beings in Him and Scripture makes that abundantly clear.

Paul makes it clear that the deal which God made with Israel - the Old Covenant - is over. The requirement to keep the Law in order to qualify for protection, provision and favour is no longer valid. When Jesus died on the cross that binding agreement was broken. However, it is important to recognise that the Law is still of value because it is eternal. The Law is eternal but the covenant that binds us to it is temporary. Verse 4 sums it up:

Therefore, my brethren, you also have become dead to the Law that you might be married to another – to Him who was raised from the dead that we should bear fruit to God.

In other words, through Jesus' death on the cross we died to the Law. We died to that marriage covenant so that we could be married to the One who was raised from the dead. The same parties are involved – God and humanity – but this time the covenant is a *new* covenant. The only way that He could work this was through death and resurrection.

I now want to take time to look at a few points here in this chapter because it goes on to talk about two different laws that are at work. These two laws are The Law of Moses (or you could call it The Law of God), and The Law of Sin that is at work in our mortal bodies.

The covenant was finished but the Law still stands. Now that the Old Covenant is finished, keeping the Law no longer makes any difference to a relationship with God. There is no guarantee of blessing for keeping the Law anymore; nevertheless, the Law itself is eternal. Jesus Himself said in Matthew 5:18:

For assuredly, I say to you, heaven and earth pass away, one jot or one tittle will by no means pass from the law till all is fulfilled.

This holds true *but* the binding covenant *to* the Law has been broken.

Paul says in Romans 7:7:

What shall we say then? Is the law sin? Certainly not!

You see, the Law, *in itself,* isn't bad. It is a good thing. Romans 7:12 even says that the Law, "...is holy, and the commandment holy and just and good!" And, in verse 14, it says that the Law "is spiritual!"

The point here is that there is nothing intrinsically wrong with the Law.

THE LAW OF GOD

Why then did God give the Law? What is the point of the Law? When the Law was given, mankind had completely lost contact with God. Generations had passed since the first man and woman had left the Garden of Eden. Humanity no longer had any capacity whatsoever to understand God or His nature and ways. Obviously people saw God as all-powerful and ruling the universe but, beyond that, what was He actually like? There was no way to know that *until* He gave the Law. From time to time God communicated with individuals such as Enoch, Noah, and Abraham, but for wider humanity there was complete ignorance of what God Himself was really like. When He gave the Law, God was effectively giving something of a description of His character. The Ten Commandments were given to help humanity understand something of the nature of God. The Law was never given primarily as a list of injunctions that were to be obeyed. Obeying the Law is the absolute minimum interpretation of it, but He had to give something so that the human race would understand what He is like.

Some years ago I was meditating quite a lot on the wording of the Ten Commandments - "Thou shalt not kill. Thou shalt not steal. Thou shalt not lie, etc." I was coming into something of an experience of the Father's love for me and coming to touch something of the quality of His love. A surface reading of the Ten Commandments didn't seem to fit with my revelation of the love of God. The harsh tone of "Thou shalt not steal!" seemed altogether too prescriptive. It was an issue of demand and behaviour!

Somehow it didn't seem right to me. The love of the Father was beginning to be very prominent in my whole perspective of what it means to be a Christian. Many years ago the Lord said to me, "James, I want you to look at everything you have ever taught. I want you to look at it again in the light of the Father's love." How do you look at the Ten Commandments in the light of the Father's love? I was beginning to be challenged about that and some things were occurring in my mind that I had no validation for whatsoever.

Not long after this we were at a gathering in Holland. There was a man there from a Jewish background. He was a New Testament scholar and his particular focus was to understand the Jewish cultural paradigm of Jesus' day. For example, how would a Jew hear some of the things that Jesus said as opposed to how we today might hear it? I was having a conversation with this man and I said to him, "I would like to sound out some of the things I have been thinking about the Ten Commandments. I have a particular perspective on the Ten Commandments but can you tell me truthfully if I am off the mark altogether? Am I totally wrong?"

He looked at me and I continued, "It seems to me that when God says, 'Thou shalt not steal' what He is really saying is 'There is nothing in Me that would steal from anybody, so if you want to be like Me, then don't steal either.' He is really talking about Himself." And, "When He says, 'Thou shalt not kill' He means, "There is nothing in Me that would harm the hair of a person's head. There is nothing in me that would commit murder and if you want to walk with Me then don't commit murder either.'" I was a bit apprehensive as I said this to such a noted Jewish scholar.

He looked at me straight in the eye and said, "James, you are absolutely right!" That was good to hear - I like to be right! He told me that in Hebrew there are no purely conceptual statements that you can make. The Hebrew paradigm doesn't deal with mere concepts. Everything is rooted in life and in relationships. These Commandments are primarily relational. So when God says, "Thou shalt not kill," He cannot simply be making a prohibition. He has to be talking about relationship.

The Ten Commandments were a way for us as fallen human beings to begin to get some grasp of what the personality of God is like. He does not steal. He does not commit murder. He knows where honour is due. He asks honour of us where honour is right. He asks us to worship Him with all our heart, mind, soul and strength because that is ultimate reality. God is bigger than us – it is foolish not to give our whole lives over to Him! All the way through these Ten Commandments (called 'Ten Words' in original Hebrew) He is describing His own personality. When we look up (and we do look up) at the Ten Commandments we are seeing a perspective of the personality of God that we as carnal and unregenerate people can understand. That's the point!

But here's the rub! Even if you keep the Law, your righteousness is *still not enough!* Why? Because that is not the righteousness that God is looking for. According to Jesus in Matthew 5:20, the righteousness that He is looking for has to *exceed* that of the scribes and Pharisees. I remember reading that years ago and thinking - *how can that ever be?* I cannot ever say, like Paul (Phil 3:6), that I am blameless in keeping the Law. Paul's self-assessment was that he never broke the Law of God. I knew that I had fallen far short of Paul's level of righteousness before I had even reached my tenth birthday! I had blown it long ago! There had to be a greater reality than that.

The Law is spiritual, holy and good because it describes something of what the personality of God is like. In *that* sense it will *always* be true and never pass away.

THE LAW OF SIN

Now, also in Romans 7, there is *another* law that is spoken of. In verse 14 and following, Paul says:

> *For we know that the law is spiritual, but I am carnal, sold under sin. For what I am doing, I do not understand. For what I will to do, that I do not practice; but what I hate, that I do. If, then, I do what I will not to do, I agree with the law that it is good.*

In other words, "When I read the Law, I agree that it is good - but I keep failing to do what is right and good. I can succeed for a day or two, maybe even a week or two, but finally it will get me. I cannot keep it!" When Paul says this, he is admitting that a deeper struggle is going on inside him. As he says himself, "I am carnal - sold under sin." He agrees (v 16) that the Law is good. But then he concedes that he cannot keep it. In his true self he desires to keep it but the sin that dwells within him keeps breaking it. He goes on to say in verse 17, "*But now, it is no longer I who do it, but sin that dwells in me.*"

To make a strong point of this, Paul repeats this very statement in verse 20, "*Now if I do what I will not to do, it is no longer I who do it, but sin that dwells in me.*" That is such a wonderful statement! It's wonderful because it frees us from guilt. It is not me that cannot keep the Law of God it is the sin that dwells in me. When Adam and Eve sinned, all of us were in them and we sinned also. Sometimes we think back to Adam and Eve in the garden and wish that they hadn't done it. I have thought if they hadn't done what they did then I would be free. The truth, however, is that we would have fallen into the same trap as they did. We all would have sinned. The whole human race became sinners when Adam and Eve fell. There is a bias in us that continually leans towards sinning. It is called, according to Paul in Romans 7:23, "the law of sin which is in my members."

There is a law, or a principle, in the members of your body, an irreversible tendency in your humanity that will continuously take you into sin. It is *within* you. Some theologians have said that you don't become a sinner until you actually *commit* a sin. In other words, you are not *born* a sinner. And they say, when you reach the 'age of accountability' you are then responsible for your decisions. After that age, believed to be around twelve years of age, when you decide to commit a sin that is when you become a sinner – but not before. That is a particular view held by a significant number of people. There is a problem with that belief, however. If that were true there must have been at least one individual (apart from Jesus, of course) in the history of the human race who had chosen *not* to sin. But not one single person from the billions of human beings who have ever lived on this planet has made the choice not to sin. If sin is a matter of choosing to, after the 'age of accountability' why is it that everybody, without exception, has chosen to sin? Because, in our human makeup, there is a bias that, when left to itself, cannot *but* sin. This is the law of sin.

These two laws are clearly defined in this seventh chapter of Romans. There is the Law of God or you could call it the Law of Moses or the Ten Commandments. It is good and we all know and admit that it is good. There is something in us that loves this law. There is something in us that demands that everyone else lives by it. Even the worst criminals in the world don't want you to steal from them. They think that theft is wrong when *they* are the victims of it. They will happily steal from others but whatever you do don't steal from them! The vast majority of criminals expect some form of fairness. Even the person who murders wants to be loved themselves. Generally speaking, a murderer does not want to be murdered. There is something deep within us that adheres to the standard of the Law even when we break it. So that is the first law. It is good and holy and no one disputes that it is absolutely right. In our minds we love the Law but in our flesh we cannot keep it. The second law is that law within 'our members' that cannot stop sinning.

I read this chapter (Romans 7) over and over for years and I absolutely agreed with Paul when he says (in verse 24), "O wretched man that I am. Who will deliver me from this body of death?" In other words, "I am continually being convicted of doing wrong things by the Law, because in my flesh I keep breaking the Law. Whether in my thinking or my actions I cannot stop myself from sinning. Even as a Christian I still keep going down that road of sinning." We all find ourselves in the same boat. It took a major failure in my life for me to see that, in all the years I had tried to live a good, Christian life by striving to discipline myself, to not sin and to do right, underneath I had not really changed. To see that underneath it all I couldn't possibly make myself a better person. I was still a sinner and all my disciplined behaviour was only a thin veneer.

This is one of the reasons why I am so against putting pastors, teachers and leaders on titled pedestals. When we have unrealistic expectations of them we are putting them in a place where they have no option but to hide the fact that they still have 'the flesh' operating in them. If we lift them up into a place where perfection is the standard to be a Christian leader, we are only setting them up for an inevitable fall, setting them up to hide their faults behind a mask of excellence and having it all together! Paul had learned to boast in his weaknesses and faults that the power of the Lord might be with him.

When we are living out of the Tree of the Knowledge of Good and Evil we think that God's blessing is directly linked to good behaviour and that bad behaviour is punished. Those who refrain from doing the bad things and who attain to the good are the ones that God will use the most. We are setting people up to be very lonely in ministry and fighting temptation that is too strong for them. I know that from past experience.

This is SOOO true!

Verse 22 says, "For I delight in the law of God according to the inward man." In this context Paul uses the term "the inward man" to refer to his *mind*. In this chapter the 'inward man' and 'the mind' are used interchangeably for they are the same thing. Paul says that he delights in the Law and loves it but he sees another law "...in my members working against the law of my mind." You can see the two laws in contrast here. This other law in Paul's members is working against the law of his mind and bringing him into captivity to the law of sin in his members. In other words, in his physical body. This is not the 'church members' he is talking about – he is talking about his own body, his appetites and actions. Due to our fallen nature the law of sin is in the physical members of our body.

He then cries out (v24) "Oh wretched man that I am. Who will deliver me from the body of this death?" How do I escape from this trap? Sin is in my body and I can't beat it! I love the law of God and I absolutely agree with it! It is wonderful – but I cannot keep it! This is the great dilemma. What is more, Jesus made it worse by saying, "You may not have committed physical adultery but if you have looked on someone with lust in your heart, it's the same thing!" Jesus said that if you are angry with somebody, it makes you a murderer! That makes the Law impossible to keep.

Paul wrestled with this terrible dilemma. He said that he didn't know what sin was until the Law came. But when the Law came (v9), "sin revived and I died." He was utterly convicted by the Law of the sin that he was committing. This is the trap. Believing what is right and good, holy and spiritual, but finding that the principle of sin operating in our members makes it impossible to keep. The benchmark set by the Law is impossible to reach. This is one of the things that causes Christians to end up sitting in a pew for most of their life – either in desperation or just hoping that they might just make it into heaven. They are caught in a trap that there is no escape from. They don't believe they can serve the Lord because they are too unholy. The Law (the Tree of the Knowledge of Good and Evil) keeps condemning them and so they live in a hopeless, joyless existence. They don't lead anyone else to the Lord because they don't want to bring them into the same trap. I can totally understand that way of thinking. I felt trapped in this as well. I felt like a wretched man unable to escape the clutches of the body of death.

THE THIRD LAW

So Paul cries this sad and powerful cry which so many of us fully identify with:

"O wretched man that I am! Who will deliver me from this body of death?"

I have cried those words in different ways many times too!

Then Paul makes this statement, which always left me with a feeling of even more frustration and dissatisfaction. He simply says, "I thank God through Jesus Christ our Lord," and then moves on.

My response to this was, "What? Did I miss something? Where is the deliverance from the trap of wanting to keep the Law but not being able to resist sinning?" How does that sentence – I thank God through Jesus Christ our Lord – open the jaws of the trap and let me walk free? I have been a Christian for years. Jesus Christ is my Saviour and Lord but I am *still caught in the trap*. Try as I might I just couldn't see any answer in all of this.

One of the problems with the Bible is that the original text has been divided into chapters and verses. These were added during the Middle Ages but we read the Bible as if they are part of the original text. Paul's discourse in chapter 7 doesn't stop at the end of that chapter. It continues right through. When he says, "I thank God though Jesus Christ our Lord," and continues, "...so then," I thought that the answer *must* be in that statement. It had to be because he appears to move on to other things.

Tell me again – how did he get free? I must have missed something. "Through Jesus Christ our Lord?" That seemed to be too simplistic an answer for me. I thought, "Paul, you've got to do better than *this*. That answer is insufficient for me. You are going to have to enlarge on that." Well, he does but it is a few lines further down divided by the beginning of chapter 8. Chapter 7 finishes off by outlining the two laws, "...with my mind I serve the law of God, but with my flesh the law of sin."

So how did he get free? As the revelation dawned on me, suddenly I realised. THERE IS A THIRD LAW. This third law is the law of the Spirit of Life!

In chapter 8:1 he says,

> *"There is therefore no condemnation to those who are in Christ Jesus...for the law of the Spirit of life in Christ Jesus has set you free from the law of sin and death."*

There are three laws! The third law, which is the key to everything, is the law of the Spirit of Life in Christ Jesus. This is the law that breaks out of the bondage of being caught between the two laws I mentioned earlier. This third law is over and above and entirely beyond the Law of Moses and the law of sin that work against each other.

How does this third law work? How does the law of the Spirit of life in Christ Jesus actually operate in our lives? When I first attempted to understand this, I thought it was talking about being filled with the Holy Spirit, that He – the Spirit of God – would give us the power and capacity to keep the law of God. I assumed that the Holy Spirit would empower me to be able to do what God requires. In other words, when you are not filled with the Holy Spirit you cannot do it, but when you *are* filled with the Holy Spirit then you have the power to keep the Ten Commandments. I believed that. The problem, however, was that it didn't actually work.

My question became – How does speaking in tongues overcome the law of sin that is in my flesh? How does it prevent me from being tempted? How does moving in spiritual gifts deal with sin? How does praying for the sick, casting out demons or even raising the dead help you to resist the temptations in your own heart? What about preaching under the anointing or worshipping in spirit and truth? Is that what gave Paul the victory over sin and the power to keep the Ten Commandments?

I was filled with the Holy Spirit a matter of months after becoming a Christian. That was over forty years ago – but I still found that I was sinning! I had experienced much of the work of the Holy Spirit in my life but my flesh was still subject to temptation. That is why it is ridiculous to think that a charismatic experience and lifestyle is enough to deal with the law of sin and fulfill the law of God. That is why even very anointed leaders still fall into moral sin. That idea has been shown to be unworkable. It is blatantly obvious that the flesh is still very authoritative. There hasn't been a third law that has been effective in overcoming temptation and sin.

What then is this 'Third Law?' Here it is! "For the Law of the Spirit of Life in Christ Jesus has made me free from the law of sin and death." What is the Law of the Spirit of Life? We could not understand this until Jack Winter had his groundbreaking revelation that the love of the Father *could be imparted*. When we realised that the love of the Father could be imparted it brought a deeper, more profound reality with it – that LOVE IS SUBSTANCE. Love is 'stuff'!

We who are in this revelation and who minister in it need to continually remember that it is *not a message* that we preach. This is a *revelation* of love that we *impart*. If we reduce it to being merely a message then it is only knowledge. But love is 'stuff' – it is actual substance.

Please understand that I am not arguing over mere semantics here. The Father's love is not a conceptual message – it is a real substance.

The Father's love is a revelation. It is an experience of the substance of the love of God being put into your heart. It is not just an understanding that He loves me. It is the receiving of the substance of His love.

THE BAPTISM OF THE SPIRIT

When Paul writes about the law of the Spirit in chapter 8, he is following on from his previous mention of the Holy Spirit. He only mentions the Holy Spirit *once* prior to chapter 8 and that is in Romans 5:5. So when we talk about the law of the Spirit, it is expressed in Romans 5:5. In that verse it says, "Now hope does not disappoint because the love of God has been poured out in our hearts by the Holy Spirit..." When we receive the Holy Spirit so often our focus is on something like speaking in tongues. When we get filled with the Holy Spirit we will receive power to do spiritual transactions like Jesus did, such as raise the dead, heal the sick, prophesy, cast out demons, and have supernatural faith. We have understood that the infilling of the Spirit is to give us the capacity to minister as Jesus ministered.

But when I saw this verse in Romans 5:5 it took me back to the day when I was filled with the Holy Spirit. The truth is, I didn't really want to become a Christian. As I understood it then, all I really wanted was to be filled with the Holy Spirit. They told me that I couldn't get filled with the Holy Spirit unless I first became a Christian. That presented a real problem for me because to become a Christian meant that I had to give my life over to someone else who would be Lord of my life. The problem was - I really wanted to retain control. My life wasn't that great but at least it was mine and to give it to someone else was scary. Because of this, it was a long process for me to surrender my life to the Lord - for Him to do whatever He wanted for the rest of my life.

Despite this misgiving, my overwhelming desire was to be baptised in the Holy Spirit. Finally, after a process of about eight months, I came to the point where I was ready to give my life to the Lord and I did so in the car as I was driving home late one night. When I woke up the next morning I walked outside. The sky turned blue and the grass turned green like I had never seen it before. It was utterly transformed in a moment of time.

I had lived outdoors for much of my life but I stood in this field in awe at the stunning clarity of the grass beneath my feet and the sky above me. I had this incredible feeling inside me. I just knew that Jesus had come into my heart. I knew beyond doubt that from that time onwards everything would be okay. I knew that it would never be like it was before, despite the tough times that would inevitably come. That was a huge experience for me and then I knew that the next thing for me was to be baptised in the Holy Spirit.

That was another long process for me. I was prayed for many times by many people for me to come to a place of committed faith to receive the Spirit. It is one thing to ask and believe. It is an entirely different thing to ask and be committed to what you are believing for. It is one thing to ask God to give you the baptism of the Holy Spirit it is another thing to be committed to that request.

One night in front of my mother and father, the Holy Spirit hit me. When it happened my Dad was so stunned that he collapsed on the sofa. His hands were down by his sides, his legs were straight out in front of him, toes pointed towards the ceiling. He was staring at his feet with a totally stunned look on his face because I had suddenly burst into tongues at the top of my lungs. It was so loud that people walking down the street must have heard me. I ended up on my knees on the floor with tears pouring down my face. I was weeping so profusely that the carpet was soaked with my tears. I was worshipping loudly in a cascade of tongues - supernatural language pouring out of my mouth. When he witnessed this, my Dad fell onto the sofa in shock and jaw-dropping amazement.

WHERE DID ALL THAT LOVE COME FROM?

In the midst of this outburst I looked across the room at my Dad and noticed that his lips were moving. He was trying to say something. I went over and put my ear close to his mouth. He was so stunned that I can't be sure that he even knew he was trying to speak. I could hear what he was trying to say. Over and over again my Dad was repeating these words, "Where did all that love come from? Where did all that love come from? Where did all that love come from?"

When I walked out of the room I was thrilled that I could speak in tongues. I wasn't thinking of love. I wasn't expecting love. I wasn't believing for love. No one had ever told me that you experience the *love of God* being poured out into your heart by the Holy Spirit. All I thought the Holy Spirit was for was to help me speak in tongues, to give me anointing and supernatural gifting. I thought the baptism of the Holy Spirit would give me that deep, holy look. I thought it was all about empowerment. I never, ever associated it with love.

When Paul is writing his epistle to the Romans, he is trying to give a synopsis of the complete Gospel to people whom he has never met. In the first eight chapters he covers the broad sweep of redemptive history – Adam, the Flood, Abraham, Israel, repentance, baptism in water and more. The only place that he mentions the Holy Spirit in these first eight chapters is in chapter 5:5. And what will happen (according to Paul here in Romans) when you get filled with the Holy Spirit is that the love of God will be poured into your heart. He doesn't mention tongues. He doesn't mention any other supernatural gifting. He talks about the love of God being poured into your heart. Anything else that we may receive is the result of that love poured into us by the infilling of the Holy Spirit.

And now, in the same letter, three chapters later he is talking about the 'law' of the Spirit. He is connecting these two things. The primary result of the infilling of the Holy Spirit is an outpouring of God's love in the heart, and this *is* what he means in Romans 8. The law of the Spirit is none other than the love of God being poured into your heart. What is going to set you free from the law of sin and of death *is* the love of the Father being poured into your heart. When His love gets poured into your heart *that will* set you free from the power of your flesh that always desires to sin.

When we look at the Law of Moses we are looking up towards God to see what His character is like. But let me ask you this question - does God keep the Ten Commandments by choice? Does He wake up every morning and resolve not to sin? No! He keeps the commandments *automatically.*

You see, the Ten Commandments are given as a description of His nature and His personality. God doesn't keep the Law by adhering to any kind of demand or principle. The Commandments are to help a fallen humanity who have completely lost touch with what He is like. Galatians 3:24 describes the Law as 'a schoolmaster' to bring us to Christ. You were never supposed to keep it. You are supposed to look at it and realise that you cannot possibly keep it. And in looking at it you cry out, "My God, please help me!"

The Law tells you that you cannot do it. It brings forth brokenness and humility. Knowing that you have sinned and broken the Law, you cry out in repentance for God's forgiveness. That was the whole point in the giving of the Law. When we look at the Law, we are looking into a description of God's personality. The major delusion has been that we are to try to keep the Law.

But let me make it very clear: what God has done by pouring His Spirit into us is that He has poured the substance of His love into us. His love is His personality. God is love. Every other facet of His personality is an outworking of love. God is good, God is kind, He is patient, He is filled with compassion, He is the God who blesses. Everything that we read about Him is an expression of love because God *is* love. He has all these attributes naturally. He is love. Love is His personality.

Now in the New Covenant, instead of giving us a commandment, He has put His personality into us. Here's the point – even if we didn't know what the Law said, when His love is poured into our hearts, we would still keep it! He kept the Law long before He wrote it! It's a part of His personality. And by the Holy Spirit He pours His nature, His personality, into us! Peter knew it when he wrote in 1 Peter 1:4:

> "By these great and precious promises *we have become partakers of the divine nature.*"

This is the law of the Spirit about which Paul exclaims, "I thank God, through Jesus Christ our Lord." This is why there is no condemnation to those who are in Christ Jesus. To "walk according to the Spirit," is to be filled every day with the love of God. When Paul exhorts the believers in Romans 5:18 to be filled with the Spirit, the original Greek gives the clear sense of continually being filled. It should read something like, "Be filled and keep on being filled with the Holy Spirit." In other words, keep on receiving His loving of you! Keep on letting Him love you. Keep on experiencing the outpouring of the Father's love in your heart. Keep on living in the love of God every minute of every day.

The substance of His love is His personality. The Law still stands; it is still right. But when we get filled with the very personality of God Himself - who is love - we go around the Law and more than fulfill it, because the Law is totally fulfilled by love. The Law will not pass away but God has elevated us from a righteousness according to the Law to a righteousness according to His own heart and His own personality.

I finally see this - knowing that He loves you, will not deliver you. Knowing that He is loving you will not deliver you from your fleshly nature. The love *itself* - the substance of it poured into your heart - will lift you *above* the Law. From His own nature of love, God formulated a law of behaviours that love automatically produces. When you are filled with that same love you will *automatically* behave like Him! This is what Ezekiel 36:27 is talking about when He says, "I will put My Spirit within you and *cause* You to walk in My ways." When you are filled with the love of God you will *automatically* love your neighbour. When you are filled with the love of God it won't be possible to lie or to steal or to commit murder. You *will* honour your mother and your father. When you are filled with the love of God you will not be able to resist loving Him with all your heart, mind, soul and strength. You will live as God lives.

LOVE CANNOT SIN

Consider the following examples from Paul's writings. These passages speak for themselves.

Firstly, in Galatians 5:14:

> *For all the law is fulfilled in one word, even in this: "You shall love your neighbour as yourself."*

Then in Romans 13:8-10:   Wow!

> *Owe no one anything except to love one another, for he who loves another has fulfilled the law. For the commandments, "You shall not commit adultery," "You shall not murder," "You shall not steal," "You shall not bear false witness," "You shall not covet," and if there is any other commandment, are all summed up in this saying, namely, "You shall love your neighbor as yourself." Love does no harm to a neighbor; therefore love is the fulfillment of the law.*

Isn't this wonderful? This isn't talking about human love, being nice to people out of our own understanding and capacity. This is being filled with the love *of God* and loving with the love *of God*. That is why it is so important to be filled with the substance of God the Father continually loving us. The actuality of His love being poured into your heart will deliver you from sin - because *love cannot sin!*

God is love and God cannot sin. Human love *can* sin because human love can be extremely self-centred. The love of God, however, cannot sin. The substance of His love poured into your heart will change your personality into the very personality of God Himself. That is the law of the Spirit! It brings Christianity down to two simple things - get washed in the blood of Jesus and be filled with the love of God. That's all there is to it! When we are filled with the love of God we cannot sin just like God cannot sin. We have totally missed the whole point of Christianity when we reduce it to issues of doing right and wrong.

I feel like I have discovered what the Gospel is. I have seen much of the expression of contemporary Christianity during my travels in the last sixteen years or so. Having travelled forty times around the world my conclusion is that the major focus of Christianity, as we know it, is the Tree of the Knowledge of Good and Evil. True Christianity, as God intends it, is when you feed on the Tree of Life that is the nature and personality of God Himself.

If you read this and you think that I am saying that you really need to believe that God loves you, you are missing the point. If you think, "I have to know that God is loving me," you are missing the point. You have to *experience* Him loving you because as that substance pours into your heart, you are free.

For many years I could only see that there were two different laws; the law of God, which is good and true, and the law of sin in my flesh. I, like Paul, was caught in the struggle between these two laws. For years I didn't see the *third* law - the law of the Spirit of life in Christ Jesus. Now that I have discovered the third law I feel as if I have come full circle in my desire to be filled with the Holy Spirit.

When I first met Jack Winter and he talked to me about receiving the love of the Father as a personal reality, my reaction was, "Christianity is not about love. It's about power and everything associated with power." I thought that Jack had missed the point and was over-emphasising the importance of receiving the Father's love. My problem was that God had clearly spoken to me to be a 'Joshua' to Jack. I knew without a doubt that it was the Lord and so I put aside many of my opinions about the Christian life to go and be a 'Joshua' to Jack Winter. I always had trouble with the concept of love. Christianity, for me, was about everything *but* love.

Finally, after forty years of being a Christian, and a lot of exposure to ministry, I have completed the circle and returned to the baptism of the Holy Spirit. The baptism, or filling, of the Holy Spirit is the love of the Father being poured into our hearts. We are looking forward to a time when God is going to pour out His Spirit across the Church. It will be a revealing of the substance of His love into the hearts of all believers.

This is the Gospel. The good news is *not* that you have to do it; the Good News is that God does it for you. When the love of the Father fills your heart you won't be able to even think of judging another. You won't have a negative thought against your neighbour. The Scripture says, in 1 Peter 4:18, that love "covers a multitude of sins." In other words, love sees the other as God made them. God looks at you with absolute love, and *love cannot sin*.

Now the trick to all this is - getting filled with the substance of His love. In Fatherheart Ministries the doorway to this is through our A Schools. Those schools aim to open the door for people to come into an experience of the love of God the Father. Where it is heading is what we believe to be the fulfillment of the Gospel. We are believing for the Gospel to be incarnated in the heart of every believer. We are believing for nothing less than the nature of God being expressed in us and in you. If this is over your head or beyond your comprehension, just wait. The love of the Father *will* fill the hearts of Christians all over the world and the sons of God will go out to every nation of the world. They will be filled with the very nature of the Father, transform Christianity, and bring about the end of this era.

I want to use the remaining chapters to explore the implications of this change in perspective. I can guarantee you that, when you begin to experience the Father's love, when the eyes of your heart become operative again, and when you begin to feed from the Tree of Life, you will notice a difference in your everyday life. The fruit of the Spirit of Life will begin to make itself manifest within you and around you. As you receive the love of the Father, Christianity will work for you and produce fruit in you, in ways that will surprise you.

PART TWO

CHAPTER FOUR

~

Transitioning from Orphaned Christianity to Sonship Christianity

The more revelation you have, the more your perspective changes. As we are coming to live increasingly in the continuous experience of God loving us and feeding from the Tree of Life, we are beginning to have our eyes opened to the reality of the Gospel. The whole purpose of Christianity basically boils down to this: Jesus died on the cross to get rid of all the stuff that stops us from coming into a life of intimacy with the Father. The point of Christianity is that we can experience the eternal life which Jesus speaks of in John 17: "...to know You the only true God and Jesus Christ whom You have sent." Many people think of eternal life in terms of linear time that goes on forever. Eternal life, however, is a quality of existence. It is a substance, the substance that causes God to be alive.

We have a very limited understanding of some of the great truths that Scripture talks about. We have reduced the Holy Spirit down to our own experience of charismatic phenomena. We are so locked into our old paradigms that when we hear the words "Spirit of God," we cannot shift from our own boxed-in views of who He is and what He does. The truth is: the Holy Spirit is the very essence and personality of God Himself!

Sometimes we need a different terminology to wake us up to the real meaning of who the Holy Spirit is. Imagine, for example, you receive the spirit of an oak tree. What would that feel like? For a start, having the spirit of a great oak tree would involve standing still for a very long time, maybe thousands of years. Imagine standing through many centuries, season after season, leaves falling off, new acorns growing…. that is what receiving the spirit of an oak tree might feel like. Or imagine receiving the spirit of a great composer. Something of the very essence of Mozart, for example, is within you and so you are going to act differently. Just take a moment and try to imagine what it would be like. You won't have to try to act differently. It will be natural as a tree producing fruit. An oak tree produces acorns naturally. Mozart composed music naturally. When we have another's spirit put inside us, we will find that we naturally start feeling and behaving like the one that spirit came from.

The spirit of a person is the very essence of their personality. Now imagine if you can, what it would be like when the spirit of God is put into you. If His spirit, the Holy Spirit, is put into you, it means that His very nature and personality is being imparted; not just the ability to speak in tongues, cast out demons or give a word of prophecy. The Spirit of God is within you for much more than that. You might see white feathers floating down from the ceiling or have gold dust on your hand as some are experiencing these days. But let me be very clear - that is *not* the essence of the Spirit of God. It may be evidence but it is not essence. The essence of the Spirit of God is the very nature and personality of God Himself. It's *His* spirit. Consequently, when we talk about feeding from the Tree of Life we are talking about being imbued with the Spirit of God. The Holy Spirit is also called 'the Spirit of life' (Rom 8:2). What life is this talking about? *Nothing less than God's life.* The spirit of the nature of God and the life of God. When that spirit gets put into you it brings the very nature of God into you. When the spirit of God gets put into you, the primary thing that happens is that love comes. Love is now available because God's nature is love and He wants to impart that love to you. When His nature of love is put into us the fruits that love produces become our personality too.

The apostle Paul understood this. He speaks about the Holy Spirit in Romans 5:5 and he says that the main function of the Holy Spirit is to "shed abroad the love of God in our hearts." This is the only mention of the Holy Spirit in the book of Romans before chapter 8. The love of God shed abroad in our hearts is a direct consequence of being indwelt by the Holy Spirit. I am just coming to understand this connection. When I first became a Christian I was told that the Holy Spirit was all about power. Now I see that He is all about love. When we are talking about the Tree of Life, we are talking about feeding on God Himself, feeding upon the expressed, poured-out nature of God into our hearts and being. We are beginning to experience this love. We are beginning to be rooted and grounded in the outpouring of His love into our hearts. As this happens, it is changing everything that we experience Christianity to be.

One of the foundational paradigms that we have come to understand is that of the 'orphan spirit.' I have written a whole chapter about this in my book *Sonship*. Put simply, when Adam and Eve were pushed out of the Garden, they became fatherless. In them, the whole human race was now cut off from relationship with God the Father and, as a result, became fatherless. The human race became infected with orphanness. This is still the basic condition of humanity. The predisposition of the human heart is orphaned. It makes no difference whether your parents were bad, mediocre or faultless. Parenting, without doubt, has a significant effect on the wellbeing of each person. But I am talking about a much deeper reality than that. I am talking at the level of the human race. Even those who have a wonderful and loving relationship with their parents are still orphaned in terms of being orphaned from the One who is their *real* Father. The whole world system is an orphan-based system. Every culture and institution in the world is basically motivated by orphanness - fear, greed, insecurity, self-preservation.

This orphanness has infected church life too. The truth is, you can be born again but it doesn't take away your orphanness. You can be baptised, filled with the Spirit, and even anointed in a ministry office but still have the heart of an orphan. You cannot cast the orphanness out of the human heart. Orphanness is not a demonic thing; it is the basic state of the human heart. This is the spirit that works in the sons of disobedience (Eph 2:2). This orphanness is so deeply rooted within us to the extent that, when we become Christians, we begin to develop an orphaned style of Christianity.

The only solution for an orphan-spirited Christianity is to encounter the fathering and mothering love of God. The intimacy of a Father loving us will break our orphan Christianity. As you come into this experience of the Father's love you will begin to see change happening in your life. Some changes may be dramatic, some may be more subtle but you will begin to experience a shifting of values and motives within your heart. Often this will take you by surprise. You won't know why some of your deeply held values and principles are changing. You will begin to lose motivation for some of the things you have done for years as a committed Christian. You may well begin to think, "What is wrong with me? I am losing my enjoyment of some disciplines I have practised for years. I no longer have the same motivation that I used to have."

As the love of the Father touches you, you come into a sense that He is totally pleased with you. You don't have to be a people-pleaser anymore. Many people are exhausted and burned out because they feel coerced to serve constantly but when they receive the unconditional love of the Father they get free. This often causes a problem in the church they are involved with. I have visited churches and spoken on the love of the Father. People have really gotten hold of it and started to walk in a life of sonship. Following that I have received complaints from pastors that people in their congregation are not willing to serve anymore. I went to one church about three times to minister, and then I didn't hear from the pastor for the next three years. One day I found myself sitting at the same table as him over a meal at a conference and he told me why I had not been asked back. "The reason I have not invited you back," he said, "...is because, when you left the last time, many of our volunteer workers came to us and said they were not going to do it anymore, and it seems to me like one of the products of your ministry is that people get lazy."

I thought that was interesting and replied, "Look at what I teach and look at what I do because I teach about coming to a place of rest, and that is one of the things that begins to happen when you come into an experience of the Father's love for you." To rest in His love becomes a very high priority; the whole striving issue begins to disappear and you begin to not want that as a part of your life anymore, I said that had certainly happened to me. The striving has gone but I am the busiest itinerant speaker that I know and the other itinerant ministers that I know all say, "James, even reading your itinerary exhausts me!" Thus, it's not about laziness but about coming into God's rest. In fact, there's an increased productivity in the whole thing.

I then asked the pastor, "Why did the volunteers quit?" He replied, "They didn't want to do the work anymore," to which I countered, "Why did you have them doing things that they didn't want to do?" He was quite offended because a lot of things in Christianity can impose a sense of obligation that you have to do something in the church. We feel a duty to keep the machine running. I don't believe that God wants you to do anything for Him that is not an expression of your love for Him. I believe He wants us to serve Him out of love and what we do is our way of showing our love for Him. If somebody is doing something for you as a family member because they feel they are supposed to, that may be fine but it's not really what you want. You want them to do it because they love you. You want your daughter to help you with the vacuuming because she loves you. You want your son to do the dishes because he loves you. I believe this is what the kingdom of God is like. A lot of things we have done in the church as a way of serving the cause and building something for God, are not done out of love at all but just as a way of keeping ourselves occupied.

There is a saying that a busy church is a happy church. Well, I can tell you how it works. A busy church is a happy church for a period of time! However, the day eventually arrives (in my experience) after about fifteen to eighteen years of hard serving, when a person begins to evaluate their life and thinks, "I am doing a lot of stuff that I don't actually want to do." They are caught in a treadmill that they cannot get off and suddenly they realise that it's not really in their heart to do what they are doing. But if a person in freedom really has a heart to do something they will probably do it for the rest of their life, the work will expand them and bear lasting fruit. The love of the Father produces freedom from the heart. Usually when a person discovers, after many years of sacrificial busyness for a pastor's vision, that they have been doing it out of a sense of duty, obligation or even (in some cases) manipulation within principles that may seem very spiritual, they simply leave the church.

I now want to highlight some of the major changes that happen when the Father's love fills your life. As your spirit begins to walk with Him as son or a daughter, these shifts will begin to occur to you and you will realise "That really is what is happening to me!"

FROM OBEDIENCE OF SERVANTS TO HARMONY OF SONS

One of these changes, obviously, is the way that we see God the Father. For most of us our only experience of Christianity has been *orphan-spirited* Christianity. That means a Christianity that does not have an experiential knowledge of the love of the Father. This Christianity has a very real relationship with Jesus as Lord, as King, as Bridegroom. Those relationships can be very, very strong of course but it is only the Father that can take away the orphan-heartedness in us. A brother cannot do that. A brother just means that we are orphans together, but it's a revelation of a Father that takes the orphan-spiritedness away.

Sometimes people will say to me "I really know the Father, I've met and experienced the Father," but I just look into their eyes and I can tell that really they just have a theological knowledge of the Father. The noted Bible teacher Derek Prince recounted how he could preach messages on the Father, believing he had a relationship with the Father because of that, and because he knew the scriptures. Late in his life, however, he came to realise that there is an experiential relationship with the Father to be entered into, and that relationship with the Father takes away orphanness. That relationship will begin to bring you into a whole new experience of Christianity.

Generally speaking, God the Father has been a distant kind of person to us. We have had a revelation of Jesus at salvation, and a revelation of the Holy Spirit in the baptism of the Spirit. That is the two-legged stool upon which our Christianity has been based. But without a revelation of the Father to your heart, the Father will remain an unknown quantity. To us, He is a distant person and we treat Him as such. The stark truth is, you cannot really break out of servant-hearted Christianity until you have an experience of the Father. That experiential relationship brings you out of being a servant into the reality of being a son.

Prior to receiving a heart-revelation of the Father, it is as if the Father Himself is a master, a commander, and a judge. Consequently our Christianity is focused on obedience to commands. Our Christianity will primarily consist of hearing the voice of God and doing whatever He says. Jesus is the one that we relate to, but the Father remains unknown. The Father is a distant and unknown person, a person that we only know about conceptually. We may even be able to hear His voice if we learn to do that, but it is a distant relationship with Him as commander and us having to obey. Our whole spiritual life will be focused on hearing orders and obeying them. Obedience is the central issue of orphan-spirited Christianity!

When we come to experience Him as a Father however, something changes. Instead of obedience, we now focus on being in harmony with the Father. You cannot be in harmony with someone that you don't know but when you come to know Him there is a shift in you. It is no longer so important to hear His commands for you; rather what matters is that He is content with you and that you are content in His love. The fear and the obligation fall away. We begin to lose that strong dominance of doing His will by command to doing His will for love. Sensing what He likes and wanting to do that. A son living in harmony with his Father.

Allow me to make a statement that is going to shock you! *Obedience is not really the issue for a Christian.* This may shock you but the fact is - God does not really want you to walk in obedience all your life. Why do I say this?

Obedience is not absolute; obedience is only relative. Obedience only has relevance when you do not want to do what you have been told or asked to do. When somebody tells you to do something you don't want to do then obedience comes into place. If I were to say to you "I want you to stand on your head for an hour" and you don't like doing that, it would be an act of obedience if you did it. It would be solely obedience because there would be nothing in it for you. You would only do it out of obedience. However, if I said to you, "Go to the shop, buy yourself an ice cream and eat it!" that's another issue. No obedience is required. You would love to go to the shop, buy an ice cream and eat it. Obedience only has its place when you do not want to do what is asked. *maybe* ... *thought provoking* —

When we first come to the Lord, our life is so removed from what God wants for us. We are so steeped in the ways of the world that when faced with God's requirement for our lives our immediate thought is, "Oh, I've never even considered that. For me to do that means I've got to stop doing this. OK, I have got a choice and for obedience's sake I will do it." But as time goes on and we come to fellowship with the Father, what happens is that His heart becomes our heart and we no longer do what He wants out of obedience, but we begin doing it because we like doing it! Rather than doing something out of obedience, I do it because I delight in it.

He is leading us to the place where we delight to do whatever He asks of us. Jesus said, *"I have food to eat of which you do not you know...My food is to do the will of Him who sent Me and to finish His work."* (John 4:31-34.) It was Jesus' delight to do His Father's will. It fed and strengthened Him as food does the natural body. As long as there is some orphanness or fallenness in us, obedience is still going to be a challenge to us. There are parts of us that do not want to do what God has asked us to do in some areas, particularly as we are breaking the hold of sin and the flesh. Obedience has its place but what He is ultimately looking for is not that we are going to be obedient for eternity or even in this life but that our heart gets changed to be like His heart. Now I truly enjoy doing what He enjoys doing and it is a matter of me moving in harmony with Him, rather than obedience to Him.

That delight in pleasing the Father can only come from a son, because only a son can be like their father. As we come into sonship, something begins to change inside us where life is not an issue of obedience any more. It is an issue of being in harmony with Him.

Instead of me now putting aside times of prayer, I find that my heart is constantly in communion with Him. When I was a young Christian somebody said to me, "Now that you are a Christian, you must have a quiet time each day." The sad thing about that exhortation was that until that point I had been praying almost all day. So when that person told me that I must set aside specific time to pray each day, later that morning I would say to myself, "Oh, I haven't prayed yet!" I began to get concerned over the specific discipline of prayer and lost the heart of prayer that was already in me. The people who created particular problems for me were the people who said that John Wesley preached his first sermon of the day at 5 o'clock every morning so we should get up early like that to pray. What they didn't know was that he went to bed at 8 o'clock every night! Those people really took away my joy and freedom as a new believer by imposing a system on me.

When you begin to grow in sonship, instead of having a quiet time every day and systematic times of prayer, you develop a *heart* of prayer. The truth is, God is not really after mere times of prayer. If He was after quiet time devotions, if that was really the ultimate in spirituality, then it would be completely impossible to obey the Scripture that says, "pray without ceasing." That exhortation is not talking about times of prayer; it means having a heart that is in His presence all the time. It is about having a heart that is aware of Him, a heart that's in prayer in a constant, more continuous way. As you come to know the Father, you find that you think of the Father and then your heart just reaches out to Him. You are developing a heart of prayer. One woman said to me "I don't feel like keeping up my quiet time regime. I just can't be bothered anymore. I am losing the discipline that I once had." She was concerned about it and my reply to her was, "Maybe you are just getting free of laws." She was getting free from a system of devotion so that her heart would be attuned to God all the time.

As I came to experience the love of the Father for me I discovered something extraordinary about God and it is this: God loves to develop a relationship with us that is completely unique to our individuality. He wants to relate to you according to your own personality. In orphan-spirited Christianity there is always a pressure to have the same kind of relationship with God as some of the big leaders in the Church or the past heroes of the faith. Many young people go on internships to try to attain to the pattern of someone else's spirituality. I have discovered that God relates to me as a hunter from the hills of New Zealand. I am not a chatty person as some people are. We go through entire days in the hills together hardly saying a word, just raising an eyebrow or exchanging a knowing look. God relates to you right down to the very details of your humanness. I have grown very comfortable with the Lord's presence and He communicates with me according to who I am.

SATAN IS THE TRESPASSER IN THIS WORLD – NOT US!

Another interesting difference between an orphan-hearted Christianity and the life of sonship is this. Many people would see that this whole world and that (in particular) we Christians have this enemy who is a major problem to us and so we have to be on guard all the time. Their thinking goes like this, *"We live in an enemy environment; there's a war to be won, there's a battle to be fought and we have to conquer Satan. We've got to kick him out; we've got a battle on our hands. We are soldiers of the army and we have a fight in front of us, and we are involved in this very serious battle!"*

so good! The Lord has taught me this already. Grateful

Many people have this perspective, so spiritual warfare becomes something that you spend much of your time learning about. There is abundance of Christian teaching and resources focused on spiritual warfare. What we keep missing is that the battle is over! We are not just conquerors, we are *more* than conquerors. We are not living on a battlefield, we are living in our Father's love, and *Satan* is the trespasser not us! Trespassing means being somewhere that you have no right to be. The truth is, we have every right to be here on this earth. This world belongs to our Dad and we are at home here.

I was talking to a pastor once about travelling in ministry, and he asked me if I'd ever been to Amsterdam. I said, "Yes, I've been to Amsterdam." He said "Oh I hate that place! It's such an evil city. That is the most evil place in the world!" He continued, "Whenever I have to land in Amsterdam, or have to go through Amsterdam for some reason, I just cannot wait to get out of there! The city is so full of evil!" I was thinking to myself, *I have been to Amsterdam a number of times and quite enjoyed it. Denise and I have wandered in different parts of the city, gone on canal boat rides. I quite like it,* so I asked him what he meant when he said that he hated it. He replied, "There are drug addicts in all the alleyways, there are drugs in the shops, prostitutes in the windows. It's just full of evil. Some of the shops are full of demons!" I thought to myself, *I might have been a bit insensitive but I've walked into many of the shops and I never saw any demons in there!*

The next time I went there I was thinking about his comments so I was looking out for what he was referring to. After a while I saw a guy sitting in an alleyway. It had never crossed my mind that he may have been a drug addict. I went into some shops, and noticed some things on the shelves that I hadn't noticed before and thought, *They are weird things to see,* and I then noticed that you could buy marijuana from the shop shelf. I am not naive. I know that there are prostitutes in the windows in some places but I didn't notice any. The reality that I live by is, "...greater is He that is in me than he that is in the world."

We don't have to fear the enemy. Our place is to walk closely with God, and God Himself looks after these things if we just stick close to Him. However, if you believe that you are *only just* able to overcome demons, then you are going to have some interesting skirmishes because, by your doubt, you are giving them strength. But when you can believe that the battle is *already* won and that you are more than a conqueror through Him who loves you, then you have the freedom of an overcomer. Wherever you go, you go in triumphal procession, carrying the conquering stance of the Lord in your heart. 1 John 4:17 says, "As He is, so are we in this world." Satan is not our enemy – we are *his* enemy!

I remember a man telling me once, "If you feel the devil attacking you, it is because your righteousness is really oppressing him and he's fighting back." It's not that he is initiating it, but the righteousness of Christ that is in you is cornering him and so he will fight back. A wild animal caught in a trap will show aggression but it is because they are on the defensive and fighting to survive. That is what Satan is like. Our stance as sons, however, is that this world is our *Father's* world. We are supposed to be here, Satan is not!

Some years ago I was speaking in a small church in Poland. It was the first time I had been to Poland and I was invited to speak to a congregation of a few hundred people. The pastor was a woman, which is a bit unusual in Poland. It is a very Catholic country, strong in advocating a solely masculine type of church leadership. The pastor had to attend to some things so I was standing there alone waiting for the service to start. Then I noticed, through the crowd, an older woman coming straight at me. Like everyone else, she was wearing a heavy coat for there was no heating in the room. She shouldered her way through the people, her eyes fixed on me. I watched her wondering what was going to happen and she walked right up to me, hit me on the shoulder and proclaimed, "I don't like you!" It was interesting, to say the least. I knew it couldn't be me that she didn't like because she was a stranger to me and anyway I am very lovable! I knew it had to be something else. I said to her "Why? What's the problem?" She said, "This is my church, I've been coming here all my life. You've only been here five minutes and you look more at home here than I have ever felt!" She was offended.

I didn't quite know how to respond but I said to her, "Well, this is my Father's house." In reality, Poland *is* my Father's country. It belongs to Him; in fact, every country belongs to my Father. Don't get too wrapped up in patriotism. The greatest nations in the history of the world are merely a speck of dust in eternity. We are part of the kingdom of God but *this world* belongs to our Father. In the past, I always looked for where I fit. Now I fit everywhere because it all belongs to my Father and everywhere

I am is home to me. This is our Father's world. Satan is the one who is out of place. We must never allow ourselves to fall into the belief that he has power over us or he has any right in our lives.

Smith Wigglesworth was one of the greater men of the last century. He was powerfully used in signs and wonders and had a very intimate relationship with the Lord. One night he woke up to find Satan standing at the foot of his bed. Not a demon but Satan himself! I guess a man in his position in those days would have warranted the direct attention of Satan. He woke up, looked up and there was Satan. What did he do? He said, "Oh, it's only you!" and turned over and went back to sleep and left Satan standing there. He didn't feel the need to rebuke him, kick him out or anything. He just said, "It's only you!" The most powerful way you can treat anybody is to ignore them.

We stand in the victory that Christ won for us on the cross. If we believe that we are continually covered by the blood of Jesus there is no need to always claim that we are covered by it! Just believe it and walk in it! The need to keep proclaiming it only reveals your doubt. Our faith is the victory that overcomes the world but if you have a faith that believes we are in the midst of a battle, then a battle is what you will get. It is according to our faith. Orphan-hearted spirituality gets caught up in these kinds of things. When you begin to touch the almightiness of the Father the authority of the enemy begins to diminish.

We knew a lady who was an intercessor and who had been involved in spiritual warfare for many years. Then she met the Father, and as time went by she began to get worried about herself. She said to us, "I'm not so concerned any more about intercession the way I was doing it before I met the Father." Let me be clear that I am not against intercessors or spiritual warfare. We have intercessors for our own ministry. I am making a particular point. This lady said that she was losing interest in spiritual warfare *the way that she had been doing it*. She said, "I wonder if I am losing my zeal for this ministry." I said to her, "I think that maybe you are just growing in faith. Perhaps you are growing in more of an understanding of who you are as a daughter of Almighty God." Our intercessory place is simply to stand. That is what Joshua the high priest (in Zechariah 3:1-5) did. Satan stood at his side to accuse him, but Joshua just stood there and the Lord rebuked Satan. Let me tell you, if you are in the presence of the Father, you will find that Satan is *already* rebuked.

FREE FROM LAWS AND PRINCIPLES
TO WALK IN THE SPIRIT

Another thing that changes when we come to know the Father. In orphan-spirited Christianity there is something about us that loves laws. Because we cannot be led by love, we try to find another way. We look for a formula to live the Christian life by. Many books today have at the end of each chapter a list of certain steps or actions, which you can take in response to what you have read. I used to read every Christian book that I could lay my hands on, now I can't get past the Bible. There's too much revelation in the Scriptures to deal with, never mind reading other books.

Much of the emphasis in our Christianity is about walking in the principles of God. I remember the little church we were in when we first got saved. It was caught up in a wonderful move of the Spirit. At the beginning of each service one of the elders would invite the Holy Spirit to come and then he would sit down. No one did anything until the Holy Spirit initiated it. The presence of the Holy Spirit was so powerful that if you stood up to do something that was not in the Spirit, your knees would shake, your voice would quaver and you would fall to the ground. The presence of the Holy Spirit was so powerful and so obvious. Then one day, and I remember it as clear as anything, a man stood up and began to preach a message on *walking in the principles of God*. As I listened to that talk I knew in my heart that the move of the Spirit was over. You see, there *are* principles of God but we don't walk in them. We walk *according* to them but we don't walk by them or in them!

We walk in the Spirit and the Spirit *always* leads us in the ways of the Lord. The Holy Spirit will never lead you outside of the ways of the Lord but let me be clear about this. Just because you walk in what the Bible tells you is right to do, doesn't automatically mean that you are walking in the Spirit. It's like the principle in mathematics; 1 + 1 = 2 but 2 is not always 1 + 1. You can arrive at 2 by an endless number of calculations, but 1 + 1 will never be anything else but 2. Walking in the Spirit will always lead you according to the word of God but obeying the word of God does not mean that you are walking in the Spirit. This is a very crucial thing to understand. There is something in our orphanness where we are always wanting to have rules and defined ways of behaving. Do this, don't do that! In our orphanness we are really scared of not having determined and exact limitations of behavior. We want to know what we can and cannot do.

Orphan-spirited Christianity is always focused on where the limits are, what I am allowed to do and not allowed to do. God doesn't actually want us to do that. He wants to set you free. As we come to know the love of the Father, and as the reality of His love grows in us, we discover that we can walk by the law of love and there is no law against it. If you walk in love you don't need any defining parameters around you. Why? Because if you love, you *will* fulfill the Law. The law of God is that He has put His love into our hearts so that we would be continually led by that love. God is spirit and He walks in love. The two issues are synonymous. It is the same for us. His love filling us by the Spirit will lead us to walk in love too.

1 Corinthians 14:1 (RSV) says, "Make love your great aim." As we walk in the law of love, striving to fulfill the principles of God becomes petty and silly. Sometimes it is so obviously silly! I'm happy for every person in the world to hear me say that! God is calling us to walk as Jesus walked and in that we fulfill the Law. If I am walking in love I will not steal from you. Not primarily because it is wrong to steal or because I am afraid of the consequences. The reason I don't steal your belongings is because *I love you.* That is the motivation for keeping the law, not because it is God's law and it is the right thing to do! I can guarantee that you will find very few people in the courts who are filled with love for the people that they have sinned against!

When you love, you will automatically fulfill the law. You will be kind, you will be gentle, you will be patient, you will be long-suffering, you will be filled with joy and you will be free.

FROM SELF-RIGHTEOUSNESS
TO AUTHENTIC HOLINESS

In orphan-spirited Christianity, we are very focused on trying to be holy. There is much talk about holiness these days. There are a number of songs about holiness. Do you know what 'holy' means? Holiness simply means 'other than.' We normally think that holiness means always doing things right and living life correctly. Holiness actually means being other than the world, different to the world system. Because God is holy it means that there is nothing in this world that you can measure Him by. He is different to everything in it.

The truth is, holiness is a very difficult to define because only God is holy. Yet He commands us to become holy so a big focus in our orphan-spiritedness is to try to become a holy person. When we become sons, it's not such a big deal in the sense that I am not so focused on being holy but I do want to be like my Dad. I want to love like Him, think like Him, act like Him and feel like Him. As His son, I want to see like He sees and understand as He understands. I want to become just like Him. When it says "Be ye holy for I am holy," what it really means is "You will be holy because I am holy, and, as you become closer to Me, My holiness will become your life!" Righteousness is not something that you do. Righteousness is a gift. According to 1 Corinthians 1:30, Jesus Christ has been made onto us righteousness from God. He has become our righteousness *and* our holiness. And as we become like Him, we become holy.

A religious striving for righteousness and holiness is replaced by the desire of a son to be like his Dad. It is less a matter of avoiding sin than a desire to be like the Father. It is a great tragedy that many people have struggled their whole life trying to stop sinning. The more that you fight sinning; the stronger its grip is established in your life, because what you focus on you become like. Rather like being caught in quicksand. The more you struggle to get free of it the deeper you are sucked into it. It's the same with fighting the enemy. The more you focus on fighting the enemy, the bigger the enemy looks and the stronger he becomes in your negative belief. What the Lord is after is not that we try to fight against sin. Of course I believe that you shouldn't sin, but the real answer is not to resist it. The real answer is to submit to God and desire in yourself to be like Him. Instead of getting rid of a negative you are building a positive. And the positive will eventually eclipse the negative.

FROM CONDEMNATION TO GRACE

One of the big problems that an orphan-spirited person has to deal with is that they think that if people don't like them it's because of the things that are wrong in them. Their first response is, "It is my fault. I am the problem." An orphan-spirited person will often try to hide their faults or put on a good face. They will display a mask of the kind of person they want you to think of them as being.

With this mindset, faults become the enemy. In fact, faults can become a very serious enemy. We think, *"If I could get rid of my faults, then everybody would love me."* But the problem with that is we can't get rid of them. We can hide them or we can live in a way that they don't show. We believe that it is our faults that stop us from getting the love we need. When we come to know the love of the Father, however, something amazing happens. My faults, rather than being my most serious enemy, actually become unimportant.

The more we come to know the Father, the less the faults are a problem. We can even boast about our weaknesses. In orphan-spirited Christianity you hide your weaknesses. Consequently, orphan-spirited leaders will not let anybody in the church really get to know them because they might discover weaknesses. As one leader told me, "If they get to know your humanity, they will see that you are just ordinary and you will lose your authority!" In orphan-spirited Christianity, weaknesses are the problem. When you show a weakness, they come down on you like a ton of bricks!

I have discovered something. When people can't have grace towards somebody's faults, it's because they are hiding their own faults. There is a pervasive attitude in the Church that we must not allow faults. We must not have faults and if you have one, suddenly it is a huge issue. However, when you come to a freedom with your faults and you can confess them, then you can just be yourself. You don't have to try to be authoritative; you don't have to try to be a leader; you don't have to try to be anybody. Just walk with God and see what He does. It is only a problem if you have an orphan-hearted ambition to be significant or simply a need to be loved. However, the experienced love of the Father fulfills all need to be significant or to do significant things. When the love of the Father fills you and overflows from you that love will do significant things of itself.

In orphan-spirited Christianity we preach freedom but, in reality, we live in bondage. We preach grace but we live legalism. It's the way it inevitably ends up. In contrast, a person who is truly free is incredibly scary. Ponder that for a while! I think the disciples were scared stiff walking round with Jesus because they had no idea what He would do next. The things that He says to the Pharisees and the Sadducees were shocking but He could raise the dead so they couldn't fight against Him. God can do anything. He is completely free. That is tremendously scary!

We are living in a time when God's fathering love is beginning to soak into us. Right across the church today we are beginning to see the love of the Father come into people's hearts. I am longing for the day when all of God's prophets and apostles are filled with the love of the Father, when all of His pastors have a fathering heart, not an ambitious heart, but are genuinely fathers and mothers to the people in this world. Orphanness is based on the wrong tree. It is always about putting a plan into action to try to please or impress God. Orphanness *is* the Tree of the Knowledge of Good and Evil. As you begin to realise that the Creator of the Universe is absolutely pleased with you and loves you just as you are it sets you free from what everyone else expects you to be. It sets you free from your own expectations of what you should be. It sets you free to rest in the certainty of the love of God in your heart, filling you to overflowing.

~

True Christian Character

When Denise and I first became Christians, it wasn't long before we began to hear messages that had a strong emphasis on developing Christian character. This was very understandable from the perspective of the leaders of the church that we were involved with. The church had been experiencing revival and its membership had grown at a very fast rate. Over a very short period of time it grew from approximately thirty people to more than a thousand. Most of the additions were new converts, and many of those new converts had come from backgrounds that were messy to say the least. As a consequence, a lot of responsibility had fallen on the shoulders of the church leadership. You can imagine if you were a church leader and suddenly a massive influx of people arrive who have just come to the Lord. Somewhere along the line you will get exhausted trying to sort their lives out, and so you try to preach on principles that will make people change more quickly. In the midst of this tremendous move of the Spirit there was still a very tight expectation of what Christian behaviour should conform to. As a result, legalism filtered through in the midst of a huge moving of the Spirit. At that time, there were unusual demonstrations of the Spirit such as thirty people receiving the same vision of the Lord at the same time. There were numerous miraculous healings and many people from very extreme backgrounds came to the Lord.

I can fully understand how the leadership of that church struggled to disciple so many new converts who needed to be "cleaned up." Because the level of anointing was so strong a saying became popular, a saying that is well known in many churches around the world. It went like this, "We don't want people with more anointing than they have character." In other words, you must develop a strong Christian character, because if you don't, then your anointing will bypass your character and you will bring disrepute to the church when your character fails. There continues to be a very strong focus in the Church today on this issue of Christian *character.*

SELF-RIGHTEOUSNESS

Let me give some examples of the things that were taught as being "good Christian character." These all come under the heading of being 'a person of principle,' a person who strictly upholds the righteous principles of God. These principles are things such as honesty, being upright, frugality, good stewardship, prudence in finances, and sexual purity; things like being cautious, and circumspect in life. The advice was, "Never rush into anything. Always think carefully before you act. Don't spend more than you need. After all, it is the Lord's money and you are only a steward of it." On that basis, therefore, you should try to get the best deal that you can. Always shop for a bargain. Drive a car that isn't ostentatious. Never be extreme - be middle-of-the-road - be careful never to do things that can be criticised. Always be diligent and make the right decision. Another buzzword in this environment was the word 'prudence.' We were counselled to be prudent, in other words, to always act according to the known facts. In a nutshell, the advice was - don't ever take a risk or live from the heart.

My problem was that, when I heard people talking like this, I couldn't stop thinking that was the last thing I wanted to be like! I felt that I was being forced into a mould that I didn't want to fit into. I wanted to be free. I wanted to live my life more spontaneously.

The truth is, I don't have any desire to be frugal. It is amazing how Christians have gained a bad reputation in the world because of this issue of frugality. I have heard of examples where certain restaurants do not want to serve Christians because the Christians do not tip the waiters generously if at all! The Christians are too frugal and tight-fisted, and notoriously bad at giving tips to the restaurant staff. They give the least amount that they could possibly give. Personally, when we eat at a restaurant, I make a point of giving more than they expect. I do not believe that frugality is a quality of Christian character. In fact, I truly believe that over-the-top generosity is a Christian character trait. God was over-the-top generous with us. He gave more than we could ever expect. He gave His Son for us. He gave His very life for us.

When you get down to the reality of what this type of 'Christian character' is, it is nothing more than *self-righteousness*. It is a rightness of living based on what *I* believe to be the correct and best thing to do.

If you start living by 'Christian principles' the question you must ask yourself is, which principles am I going to live by? Which ones have the priority at any particular moment? In a given situation, should you be frugal or should you be generous? Which principle is operative here? We make the decision ourselves instead of following the impulses of the love of God. We choose to use a principle instead of allowing love to determine our actions. If love is to be the basic foundation of our lives then working out the correct principle to live by is back to eating from the wrong tree – what is the good thing to do? What is the bad thing to avoid? We are not to walk by evaluating which principle we should use at a given time according to our current understanding, which is flawed. We are to be led by the Spirit, which is the nature and the love of God within us.

This issue of 'good stewardship' has been and continues to be a huge issue in the Body of Christ. This gives absolute licence for greed and covetousness, and for holding tightly onto what you possess. It gives permission for you to make sure you keep the best for yourself and being very cautious about giving beyond that. According to 'good stewardship' it is tantamount to a sin to give away more than your means; it is wrong to give away too much. Good stewardship limits you to only giving from what is left over after you have fulfilled your responsibilities. You only ever give out of your disposable income. When we actually look at this we will find that over and over in Scripture, that sort of attitude is condemned. In 2 Samuel 24:24 we read the words of King David to Arunah the Jebusite, "No, but I will surely buy it from you for a price; nor will I offer burnt offerings to the Lord my God with that *which costs me nothing.*" When Denise and I read that passage we determined that we didn't want to give to the Lord only out of our excess. We want to give to the Lord something that has cost us. If you are only giving out of your excess – and you never do otherwise because of 'good stewardship' – then it goes against the leading of the Spirit when moving in realms of supernatural faith.

The widow who put her two coins into the temple offering did not give much in terms of monetary value. It was a very small amount of money but she gave all that she had. Of all the people who have ever given money in an offering, her story is the one highlighted by Jesus and recorded in Scripture. It's interesting, isn't it? According to the principles of 'good stewardship' that poor widow did the wrong thing! There is something about her putting in all that she had that is akin to the heart of God, who put in all that He had. Romans 8:32 brings this out: "He who did not spare His own Son, but delivered Him up for us all, how shall He not with Him also freely give us all things?" Because He gave His best there is nothing that He will withhold from us.

True Christian character is actually God's own character being imparted into us so that we become like Him. Things like being careful, circumspect, prudent, and having sobriety are all self-determined where I determine by my own evaluation what is the right way to live.

I have found oftentimes that visiting speakers get the minimum possible when it comes to getting honorariums. We have found many churches to be very generous to us but all too often churches elsewhere exercise 'prudence' and hold back when it comes to paying an honorarium. This is not the heart of God. Many churches are focused on giving what is the least amount they can get away with. Personally speaking, I would rather give too much than not enough. I believe that is closer to the true heart of God. The parable of Luke 15 has been described as the 'parable of the prodigal son' and yet it is more accurately the story of 'the prodigal father'. It was the *father* who was over-the-top in his generosity. Rather than being about a son who spent too much, this story is about a father who loved too much - if you could say it like that. I would much rather give someone more than they expect.

Real Christian character is not about being a 'good steward' in terms of holding back in giving or spending. It is about being a good steward by giving *more* than is necessary because that is what the character of God is. We know about 'Christian character' as it is in the wrong tree. We are very familiar with it in the knowledge of good and evil. But what does Christian character look like in the love of the Father? How does the Father's love outwork itself in the life of a son or a daughter? How would He want us to live out our lives?

I want to explore some issues that I believe are the foundations of what Christian character really is. This is what the love of the Father will release you into. These are some of the fruits of being loved by the Father.

DISINTEREST IN REPUTATION

The first one is something that was a major characteristic of Jesus' life. It is **a complete disinterest in reputation.** The first thing that Jesus did in coming to earth was that He left the glory of heaven and became a man. He laid aside His glory and His reputation to come to earth, and while He was here on earth, He had no interest at all in anything that could give Him a reputation. When they sought to make Him a king, He escaped from their midst. He moved away from the adulation of the crowds to seek out the desert place. In fact, when He was crucified, He was counted among the criminals. He died, hanging naked on a cross. He didn't die with a cloth round his waist as the medieval artists depicted to spare the blushes of those who sponsored them. No! He was stripped naked and hung on the cross in the view of many onlookers. He took the place of shame. We can look at that and think that He suffered shame so that we don't have to. No way! He did it as an example for us to follow. As He walked in the world so are we to walk (1 John 2:6).

He has shown us the way to live. He is *the* Son of God and we are learning to be sons of God like Him, our elder Brother. I used to think that making Jesus my Lord meant that He was my Commander and whatever He told me to do I had to obey. When He shouted an order I had to snap to attention and run to obey the order. I have since discovered that is not really what it means. He *is* the King - but we are not citizens and subjects of the Kingdom. Because we are in Him (the Firstborn of many brothers and sisters) we are already members of the royal family. All the attitudes of Jesus are to have dominion and lordship over our attitudes. We are to become *like* Him. When we talk of the lordship of Jesus it means that all that He is to determine all that we will become. And everything in us that is not like Him must submit to Him. I am to live out the same values that He has.

When Jesus says, "I am the Way, the Truth, and the Life. No-one comes to the Father but by Me," He is not only saying that His death on the cross opened the way for us to come boldly to the Father. He is saying, "*I* am the Way." In other words, if you want to come to the Father and know the Father more deeply, live as I live! Because this is how He lives and this is the person the Father enjoys fellowshipping with.

The Father fellowships with someone who has made himself or herself of no reputation. Your desiring of reputation and wanting others to think highly of you gets in the way of intimate fellowship with your Father. When Jesus said, "I am the Way," He also meant, "Become like Me!"

Jesus made Himself of no reputation and what is more, He continuously chose the pathway of destruction of reputation. Travelling like I do, I am faced with the same issue in some interesting ways. I have had opportunity to meet some of the most prominent leaders in contemporary Christian circles. I have had meetings with some very influential people. I have invitations to speak at places where, if I am accepted there, it could open up very big opportunities for me to do further ministry.

I remember speaking to a group of leaders in one of the major churches in Asia. The membership of this particular church was in the tens of thousands and I was addressing about seventy of their key leaders. As I stood in front of them the thought passed through my mind, *'If I do a real good job here...'* and I began to imagine the doors that could potentially open up for me. Then the thought came to me, *'What are my options? Do I preach what I know they would like to hear so that I can get access to a congregation of twelve thousand people?'* Thankfully, this happened more recently and I was very aware of this issue of seeking reputation so it did not present a serious temptation to me - but those thoughts *did* pass through my mind.

Or, to give another scenario, I am sitting at a meal with some of the well-known names of the Christian church today, and the temptation is to think that if I make a favourable impression, then certain opportunities will open up for me. When they are organising a conference they might invite me to be one of the keynote speakers!

The more that you know the Father's love for you, the less you have to overcome the fear of man. You won't have to try to stop being shy any more because what people think of you becomes less and less relevant. If someone has a negative opinion you can give them freedom to have that opinion yet stay free because of this overwhelming sense of the Father loving you. When somebody as wonderful as Him loves me, then why should I take notice of someone who is negative about me? Why should I take that to heart? Now there are times when somebody will say something and we need to go and say, "Lord, is this true?" Often God can be speaking into our life through what they are saying.

The orphan spirit is very focused on getting the approval of others, so we live in the fear of what people think of us. In our hearts we strive to get respect and a sense of self-worth. Let me just say this – when you experience the Father loving you, you will naturally feel worth something. You will naturally feel valuable. You won't have to go through a self-worth programme. Anything that helps is good, but ultimately the help we need is the revelation of the Father's love for us. Sometimes people need help where they are at so I am not criticising the usefulness of some these initiatives, but when we come to experience the love of the Father some of these things are going to be swallowed up. The love of the Father is going to go much, much further than the interim solutions that are offered. I love what my wife, Denise says: "The love of God does not follow value or worth. It creates it!" He doesn't love you because you are valuable, but His love will reveal the value in you and you will feel valuable.

The truth is, the desire for a good reputation is of our fallen humanity. We want people to think well of us. The level of insecurity in you will determine the level of temptation that you are vulnerable to. But let's face it - you *could* do what everyone else wants you to do, but you wouldn't enjoy yourself, would you? It wouldn't be the real you. You would muck it up anyway!

This issue of what others think, this desire for reputation, keeps us from fellowship with the Father. The Lord has absolutely no self-interest. He is not remotely self-absorbed. The Trinity is absolutely focused on each Other and on us, the objects of Its love. That is why Jesus did not value His reputation. He loved His Father so much and He loved us so much that He did not hesitate to lay aside His glory:

> "...who, being in the form of God, did not consider it robbery to be equal with God, but made Himself of no reputation, taking the form of a bondservant, and coming in the likeness of men. And being found in appearance as a man, He humbled Himself and became obedient to the point of death, even the death of the cross."
> - PHILIPPIANS 2:6-8

When Jesus looks at you He is utterly absorbed with you. That's what love is.

This is a major issue in our Christianity. I believe this is where the love of the Father is taking us. The more you are aware of Him loving you, the less you will really care what other people think of you. Many times we say, "I don't care what people think of me," when we actually care very much. Often we try to be brave and deny our hurt feelings and insecurity, but it is another thing to have no interest in what others think of us. To be so convinced in who you are and what God has called you to do that you are disinterested in the criticism or praise of others is a place of true security. When I used to look at people who emphasised 'good character' so strongly, my evaluation was that they not only appeared boring, but there seemed to be little anointing on their lives. Anointing goes alongside something that is a little wild. Anointing is not predictable. You have to be free of what the world expects of you to be able to move with the wind of the Spirit.

A HEART TO BE A BLESSING

The next major foundation of true Christian character that I want to highlight is - **having a heart that wants to *be* a blessing**.

In sonship, it is not so much about the desire to be *blessed* but the desire to be *a blessing*. A servant is always looking for profit and growth in their life. A son learns to lay down his life. As we are coming into sonship this issue will arise to challenge us again and again. To a servant-hearted or orphan-spirited Christian, the focus is on profit. To a son, the focus is on the Father because the Father becomes real to you. The more real the Father is to you, the more you want to be a blessing. A shift begins to happen in you so that it doesn't matter so much whether your stuff is getting sorted any more. It is about what is right for Him.

This is a major issue when it comes to ministry. Many people are consumed with "*my* ministry", what God would do with *me*. I was talking to a pastor in the USA a few years ago and he had a young leader in his ministry who he regarded as a wonderful youth leader, yet he was really disappointed. He disclosed that this youth leader, while still on staff in the church, had now created his own ministry name. He had his own website and was all about promoting himself and his ministry for the future. This guy was going to build his own ministry and in his heart had already left the older man. In contemporary church culture we are obsessed with our own personal ministry. Thousands attend prophetic conferences to get a prophetic word about their ministry or their future. However, it has always been God's way to deal more with a remnant than the crowd. In orphan-spirited Christianity we see each other as competitors or rivals. Jealousy and envy is rife within the Body of Christ because ambition is a big issue for us. Many people are pursuing what they want to do 'for God' but very often it is a backhanded way of *what can I get out* of what I do for God?

This can apply to leaders too. Leaders can be so insecure that they will not raise up other leaders under them. They send them out and get rid of them so that there is no competition for leadership within the organisation and no one to threaten the status of the leader. If some person begins to rise up and show gifting, leaders who are orphan-hearted will combat it. I think we all know what I am talking about. Sometimes leadership says, "If we keep the congregation young and don't grow them up, there is no threat to us." That is an orphan-spirited issue working there. I don't know that it is always consciously done but it happens within orphan-spirited Christianity a lot. One of the things I have discovered is that, if you want to have a ministry, then put all of your effort and time into helping others find theirs. If you put all of your time into finding your ministry, I can guarantee you one thing: you will never find it! You will never expand into anything. Nothing will happen as far as ministry is concerned if your focus is to find a ministry for yourself. However, if you put all your effort into helping others come into what God has for them, you will find a ministry for yourself. Your ministry will be serving others and that is what ministry means. Ministry means serving but we have often turned it on its head to mean something entirely different.

I recently came across something that Derek Prince wrote concerning Philippians 2:3. Paul there warns us as servants of the Lord that nothing be done through selfish ambition or vain conceit. That is what verse 3 says, but then Derek Prince makes the comment:

> *"Over the years I have observed that one persistent, pervasive problem in the church is personal ambition and competition with other ministers. Let me add that I observed this first and foremost in my own life."*

I love him for that! I have observed it in my life too and I think that it is part of the orphan state. In the orphan state everyone is in it for themselves. Look after 'Number One' because no one is going to give you anything! That is the orphan motto. But in sonship it is different. There can be jealousy and envy of the older brothers that arises out of our orphanness, but when we know the Father and His loving us we become family! Then 'brothers and sisters' become much more than just a title we use for people. It becomes a privilege to have a brother who is older than me. In orphan-spirited Christianity there is no benefit to have brothers older than you because they will take what is yours. In sonship, however, older brothers and sisters become a blessing to us because they have things that we don't have and we can benefit from that.

If you have merely the heart of a servant towards God you will also have an expectation of reward. You will expect to be blessed for doing what you are told. This is very prevalent in today's Christianity. There is a strong emphasis on God looking after you if you are faithful to do His will. There is a culture of deservedness operating within the Body of Christ. Some people even say, "If I am a son of God then I deserve to always travel first-class and stay in the best hotels." Servant-hearted Christians always expect to be blessed. A son, however, is motivated to bless his Father. In the final end the greatest blessing you can have is a Christlike personality. This is something that the love of the Father will lead us into. With His love in your heart you will begin to care more for others more than you care for yourself. You will come to desire the success and blessing of others above your own.

Years ago, Denise and I made a decision. We had been in the ministry a long time and our focus and prayers had always been for God to bless us, bless our ministry and what *we* were doing. Then I heard someone praying that again, "Lord, bless our meeting tonight. Add Your blessing to what we do," and something inside me responded, "I have had enough of this! I have had enough of asking God to bless *me* and *my* ministry!"

Now, when I go to speak, I am often asked to join the pre-service prayer meeting. I avoid these prayer meetings! I do so for two reasons: Firstly, because I can't handle that much unbelief, people mostly praying from earthly hope, pleading with God to do something rather than expectant faith. The other reason I don't go is that I am tired of asking God to bless *us* - bless the meeting, bless the worship, bless the preaching! I don't want Him to bless *me* any more. From now on, I want to be a blessing to *Him*. Whether He blesses me or not, I want to bless Him. I just want my life to give *Him* pleasure.

This is powerful to me

142

That change of attitude has been incredible for us. As long as you are wanting God to bless *you*, you will always try to fit God into what *you* are doing. But when your desire is to be a blessing to God, He will include you in what He is doing. There is a huge difference between these two attitudes. I have had so many people say to me, "We have been working for the Lord all these years and we still don't have such and such," or "We've been serving the Lord for years and 'this' has not happened yet for us!" It is as if, because we have been serving Him so faithfully, He should have provided these things for us. That is a servant's mentality. A servant works for a reward. A son works in harmony with his father to be a blessing to the father's heart.

In servant-hearted Christianity there is a notable absence of the spirit of the martyrs. Ponder that for a moment! When our attitude is about what we will get from it, about 'me' getting blessed and that God *should* be doing such and such for me - this is not the pathway of the martyrs. The pathway of martyrdom is to be a blessing to Him - even to the point of losing your life. If your death is a blessing to Him then let it be so. That is the attitude of the martyrs. The spirit of the martyrs is not on getting oneself blessed. It is to lay down your life to *be a blessing*. Our Christian culture in the Western world has largely forgotten this.

In all my travels, only a few times have I smelt the fragrance of the spirit of the martyrs in ministries that I have been with. But when I have experienced it, it is a wonderful thing. I remember once in Fiji, I met three young women who were living on a hillside building a ministry centre for the Indian cane cutters who were virtually slaves. They couldn't own their own land and when they tried to improve their living quarters, the landlords would move in and throw them out. They were trapped in a vicious cycle of hard manual labour under the plantation owners who never gave them any breaks or opportunities for betterment. When I visited them, these girls were digging a pit for a latrine. They were down the pit about eight feet, using pickaxes to break the hard rock, filling buckets which they hoisted to the surface with a rope. They were working in conditions of searing heat and humidity. When they saw me, they climbed out of the pit and invited me to share lunch with them. They had soup, which was basically hot water with a few leaves or blades of grass floating in it. But you should have heard them give thanks! They went into a time of worshipping the Lord, their hearts bursting in gratitude for what God had given them. I sensed there was something in them that the martyrs would have felt very much at home with.

The Church is built on the blood of the martyrs. Some nations will not have any breakthrough in the Spirit until the blood of martyrs is shed. The blood of martyrs is one of the major weapons used by God to crack open a nation to the Gospel. The desire of wanting to be a blessing rather than to be blessed is in the spirit of the martyrs and in the spirit of sonship.

CREATORS OF JOY

Another major foundation of Christian character in the Father's love is to be **a creator of joy**.

People who have real Christian character create joy. Their presence brings joy. We have been under the illusion that Christians have to be very serious people because Christianity is a *serious* business. Some Christians even consider it a sin to laugh. I have heard it preached. The preacher says something like, "Here we are laughing but do you think God is sitting up in heaven laughing at the problems of the world? Do you think *He* is laughing at the wars, famines and tragedies in the world?" That sort of comment certainly kills any joy!

It is easy to get caught up in thinking that the only response to a fallen world is to be serious. I remember hearing Heidi Baker talking about this very thing. She lives and works in Mozambique, one of the most destitute nations of the world. She ministers to people who have experienced horrendous events in their lives. One of the things she does is just holds babies in her arms as they die, giving them love in their final few hours. She said, however, that in the midst of such suffering, she was so full of joy that she wondered to the Lord how it could be? How could she have such joy in the midst of such suffering? I don't remember all that the Lord answered her but one thing stuck in my mind. He said to Heidi, "What these people need is joy. These people need a reason to be happy. They don't need people who are only serious. They need people who can create joy in them."

One of the things about being a mother is this – many mothers will live at the same emotional level of that of their saddest child. In a given day, whichever child in the family is the unhappiest, the mother will be at the same emotional level. When that child gets happy again, the mother will transfer her attention and identify with the next saddest child, so she will continually live at the lowest emotional level in the family. Yet what children really need is a mother who will lift them out of their sadness to her level of happiness. Many Christians live life like this. They live life at the lowest possible level of joy there is.

What the world needs is joy. I really believe that true Christian character is the capacity to create joy.

I totally agree with this!

When we first became Christians I was a very different person to the person I am today. We had been Christians a couple of years and I often felt extremely lonely. I no longer had anything in common with my old hunting buddies and I had no Christian friends. The church we attended had grown rapidly from about thirty members to over a thousand. Sometimes when we went to church we were welcomed at the door as if we were there for the first time. People who we remembered when joining the church didn't recognise us and would welcome us at the door as if we were newcomers! I was shy, hurt, and unfriendly. I bemoaned to Denise once that I didn't have any friends in the church and she said back to me, "James, it would really help if you smiled from time to time!" I had no capacity within me to smile. Joy had to come from a place in me that desperately needed healing.

We lived in the countryside about thirty miles from the church. In the first two years of being Christians not a single church member visited our home. Many people from the church visited other church members who lived a mile from our house, but we got no visitors. We were so much into everything of God and threw our whole energy into the church, but we felt no one was really interested in us.

Then one day, I saw a car coming down the gravel track that led to our house. To my surprise it pulled into our driveway and a man got out. It was a guy called David Pickering. David was one of the deacons of the church. He knocked on the door and I answered it. David's eyes were shining brightly and he burst out, "You guys are so lucky to live here! What a beautiful setting to live in!"

He stepped into the hallway and took the cup of tea we offered him. "Wow!" he exclaimed. "Did you guys put this wallpaper on the walls? That is fantastic wallpaper! You have such great furniture!" Everything he looked at he commented on with such enthusiasm that we began to take another look at our possessions and the house. When he left I felt as if we were living in a palace. His visit lifted our spirits tremendously and had a huge impact on us that day. He created joy. He was the most exuberant person you can imagine. During worship at church he would bounce around - springing rather than dancing! He brought that exuberance into our lives that day and put a smile on our faces and thankfulness in our hearts.

Christianity is not about seriousness and caution. It is primarily about joy. If a person doesn't have joy, they are still very immature in Christian character. It is not only having joy that matters; it is having the capacity to impart the joy that tells us we are beginning to come into a place of effective Christian leadership. Paul talks about being "...helpers of your joy." (2 Cor 1:5 AV) That is what preaching is about. Preaching is to help people rejoice. The aim of preaching is to create joy. There isn't any point in preaching otherwise. We are to help people get free of stuff so that they can greatly enjoy their life and their walk with God. Imagine a church whose sole focus is to increase the absolute enjoyment of God in people's lives. Christian character and ministry is about bringing people increasingly into joy. When you think about that, it is obvious.

We have a friend from South Africa, who got filled with the love of the Father. He was both pastor of a church in his town as well as the mayor. As a pastor he found that his church wasn't growing so he asked the Lord how to get the church to grow. The Lord told him to join the local rugby team. Knowing that he was a Christian, the other players in his team believed he was a soft touch even though he played in the toughest position in rugby. Then, during one game, his opposite number in the other team targeted him. To his team's surprise, Kobus retaliated and punched the guy. That incident gained him the respect of his teammates and they all came along to his church.

Kobus came to one of our meetings in Pasadena, California, and was very impacted by the Father's love. This experience really changed him and his preaching in his home church changed radically as a result. On the third Sunday after his return from Pasadena one of his church members approached him after hearing his sermon. The man said to Kobus, "I am not coming to this church any more. I am going to attend another church in town." Our friend asked him, "Why?" and the guy answered, "Well, when I used to come here I would always leave feeling guilty. But now that you are preaching this 'Father's love stuff' I don't feel guilty any more, so I am going to find a preacher that makes me feel guilty!' How twisted an idea of Christianity is that? That type of Christianity is about the impossible task of trying to bring people to holiness by guilt and condemnation.

I don't believe that Christianity is about the ability to impart guilt. Sometimes I see a preacher advertised as "a very challenging speaker" or having "a challenging message." I never want to hear another challenging speaker. We have enough challenges. We don't need any more challenges. We need power and joy to meet the challenges that life throws at us. I don't want to come out of church thinking that I must do better - I *must* - I *should* - I *have to*. I don't want to be challenged to do things - I want to discover who *God* is and what *He* has done. Because when I discover what *He* has done, something in me responds to Him. When I discover who He is, something in me cannot help loving Him. Years ago, as a young preacher, the Lord spoke to me and said, "James, never tell people what they must do or what they have to become. Tell them *who I am* and what I have done!"

So much of Christianity today is telling people what they must do and what they have to become. So often I hear lines like, "If the Church was really doing its job," "if we were really the people we are supposed to be" or "This is what God requires of us. It's up to us to change the world for Him." When I hear comments like that I am not remotely interested. I don't know about you but I am not a world-changer. I am just a guy that God found in the gutter. There's no 'world-changing' potential in me. I'm not a 'history-maker' either. I didn't buy into making history or changing the world; I just bought into being saved because I desperately needed it. I bought into a God who would love me and help me with the mess of my life. I didn't come into Christianity to make a big impact on the world.

Yet, what I have discovered is this: as I surrender more and more to God's love, He occasionally changes a small part of the world *through* me. It has nothing to do with me. While speaking at a conference once, I said that about not being interested in being a 'world-changer' or a 'history-maker', completely unaware that the next conference they had organised was called *World Changers and History Makers!* Needless to say, I wasn't invited back.

It sometimes distresses me to see young people being pushed into a zeal that is only based on human enthusiasm. That is not the true Christian pathway. I know where that ends up. The truth is, I have already been down that path and it led to disillusionment and despair. I *did* burn out for God. It wasn't all it is cracked up to be. In fact, it was a horrendous experience and I learned that burnout wasn't what God wanted. Only the flesh can actually burn out. If we are in the Spirit, we will be at rest and still be fruitful. The truth is, we are supposed to go from faith to faith and from glory to glory, being continually changed into His image. Christianity is about becoming like Jesus, and a large part of that is to be filled with joy.

One of the major issues of Christian character is to be greatly enjoying your life and your walk with God. If you are living your life in a straitjacket of good behaviour you will certainly not enjoy it.

CONTENTMENT

True Christian maturity is marked by **contentment**. This characteristic is foreign to many people yet it is the most sought after quality of a person's life. This is not so much about happiness. Happiness can come and go but contentment is the peaceful acceptance of where I am in my life - this is who I am, this is where I am presently at, and I am content to be like this. Paul talks about this in Philippians 4:11 & 12:

> *...for I have learned in whatever state I am, to be content: I know how to be abased, and I know how to abound. Everywhere and in all things I have learned both to be full and to be hungry, both to abound and to suffer need.*

There are still areas of my life that I am not happy about, but compared to where I used to be I have changed significantly. I believe that God is wanting to bring us to a place of contentment. Contentment is really one of the major issues of Christian character. We need to understand that contentment doesn't necessitate everything being right in our lives. On the contrary, it is about having peace when things are less than perfect and are not going right, and where there are wants and needs. Paul learned to be content in the midst of great need and difficulty.

I really believe that we cannot have this contentment apart from an experiencing of the love of the Father. His love is really the only thing that ultimately transcends the issues of this world. When the reality of the Father's love begins to eclipse your own emotional responses to the problems that this world throws at you, you will find contentment beginning to establish itself in your heart.

I believe that we are to minister out of a place of contentment rather than using ministry as a means to make us content. Jesus said, "Blessed are the peacemakers!" A peacemaker is a person who is so full of peace that it leaks out all over the place. When that person walks into a room, peace descends upon it. You must have peace to be able to bring it. Peace changes the atmosphere. The spirit of a believer will expand out into the atmosphere around them. The fruit of the Spirit is an aggressive weapon of our warfare. We often think of the weapons of our warfare as the sword of the Word of God. But it is that Word made flesh in us that is effective in warfare. When you have so much joy in you that circumstances cannot dampen, you are overcoming the enemy. When someone is really angry with you and you are totally at peace in your heart you will disarm that anger. Contentment will defeat the temptation that Satan offers to ensnare you.

Sonship is manifesting the Father so that people actually touch the reality of the Father through us. Not only is contentment wonderful for your own life but also it will affect others bringing them into peace and rest. Contentment is an aggressive weapon of our warfare against the enemy. The greatest weapons in spiritual warfare are things like peace, joy and contentment. This is the Word becoming flesh in our lives. I see too much restless, driven activism in the Church today. Plans, visions, purposes, callings and ministries that are often just the frustrated outworkings of discontented hearts. We need to bring Paul's contentedness to the Church. When the Church comes into the same contentedness and rest that Paul ministered from, it will begin to achieve the same results as Paul.

THE FATHER'S VALUE SYSTEM

The real issue of Christian character is this; what is God's nature like? True Christian character is a matter of displaying God's nature, becoming like Him by embracing Him in our hearts. Orphanness is basically insecurity – and the insecure hold onto things like reputation and money for security. I believe this is what Jesus' parable of Luke 12:15-21 is referring to:

> *And He said to them, "Take heed and beware of covetousness, for one's life does not consist in the abundance of the things he possesses." Then He spoke a parable to them, saying: "The ground of a certain rich man yielded plentifully. And he thought within himself, saying, 'What shall I do, since I have no room to store my crops?' So he said, 'I will do this: I will pull down my barns and build greater, and there I will store all my crops and my goods. And I will say to my soul, "Soul, you have many goods laid up for many years; take your ease; eat, drink, and be merry."' But God said to him, 'Fool! This night your soul*

will be required of you; then whose will those things be which you have provided?' "So is he who lays up treasure for himself, and is not rich toward God."

That man was saving up for his retirement and the Lord said to him, "You fool!" That is pretty strong language. Money *is* important, but it is important for what *God* wants it for, not just what insecurity and orphanness would do with it.

When we read of Jesus honouring the widow who gave the two mites, what we are really seeing is the value-system of the Father. If we walk in the way that Jesus walked - according to the Father's values and desires - then our capacity for intimacy with God the Father is increased. The same principle works in our own human lives. For example, when I was younger I loved to play table tennis. I found that I spent more time with people who enjoyed playing table tennis. Those who have the same interests as me automatically hang out with me more than those who don't have similar interests. The point I am making is that our common interest and value in the game of table tennis encouraged fellowship together. In the same way, understanding what gladdens the Father's heart will develop intimacy with Him. If you have something in your heart that is inconsistent with your heavenly Father's values, there will be a shadow in your intimacy with Him. But when you and He are in harmony, you will experience fellowship with Him. That is how sonship operates. If you are generous you are going to experience closeness to your Father, who is generous too. If you are frugal and a penny-pincher you will not experience identification with your *prodigally lavish* heavenly Father. Whenever money issues arise you will not be in harmony with Him.

WALKING IN THE SPIRIT

I invite you to exorcise from your thinking that old orphan-hearted, servant-hearted paradigm of what Christian character is. If you adhere to that old mindset it will bind you to reputation, to constantly monitoring your own self-development and trying to live life by your own human efforts. The subtle danger of this is that, even if you have God as your goal, you are living by human effort. Living by Christian principles is actually living from the Tree of the Knowledge of Good and Evil. The truth is, we are to walk by the Spirit *not* by principles. If you live by Christian principles you will end up in deception because you are not living in relationship with God.

Neither are we to walk "in the Word." We are not to obey the Bible just because the Bible says something. We walk *according* to the Word but we walk *in the* Spirit. If the Word condemns something then we know that we are not walking in the Spirit – but obeying the Word is not the same as walking in the Spirit. Walking in the Spirit will always be according to the Word, but the converse doesn't hold true. Because you live by the Word it doesn't necessarily mean that you are in the Spirit. Walking in the Spirit will *always* lead you to live according to Scripture, but the reverse is not necessarily the case at all. I know many people who claim to be faithful to the Word but who have no idea what the Holy Spirit is saying.

What is 'walking in the Spirit?' It is the love of God being poured into our hearts. As we walk in that love of the Father continually being poured into our hearts, *that* is walking in the Spirit. That is the life that Jesus lived. This is the law of the Spirit of life in Christ Jesus. May we have the capacity to see what it is to walk as Jesus walked – to be free of principles, instructions and rules. May God set us free from that domination of expectation to truly be His sons and daughters. The glorious freedom of the sons of God is outside of confines, structures and prisons of principles and laws, no matter how right they may appear. He wants us to be free to dance with Him for it is only love that is completely free.

Something struck me once that was both surprising and liberating. I had been strongly influenced by many Bible teachers that to live the Christian life successfully I had to do what the Bible (especially the New Testament) said. But the fact is, none of the Apostles ever read the New Testament – not even once. They didn't live their Christian lives by obeying the Word. They didn't read the New Testament – they wrote it! They walked in the Spirit and the Spirit led them to live and learn many things. Those things they wrote down and that subsequently became the New Testament. Walking in the Spirit of God will also cause us to walk according to what they lived. And the love of God that spilled out of them will overflow from us too!

CHAPTER SIX

~

Overcoming the World - The Battle for the Emotions

As we are coming to experience and walk in the love of the Father, our perspective of Christianity is changing profoundly. God is restoring to us the reality of what Christianity truly is. I want to look at a particular verse that I never really understood and it would frustrate me a lot. It is the last verse of John 16. This was probably the last teaching of Jesus' earthly life, prior to His crucifixion, so it was very important. It is followed by His prayer to His Father but these are effectively the final teaching words to His disciples. He says:

> *These things I have spoken to you that you may have peace. In the world you will have tribulation, but be of good cheer I have overcome the world.*

When I used to read this I would have problems with it. I didn't dispute Jesus saying, "In the world you will have tribulation" - I agreed with that absolutely! That statement is so true! Let me let you into a secret - tribulation will never stop. You *will* have problems in this world. I have been in the Christian life for more than forty years and I can tell you it has been true throughout my Christian life but it is much better to go through these things with the Lord than without Him. Even knowing that He exists is a help. Notwithstanding that, there are still going to be problems. When Jesus declares that you will have tribulation in the world, He means that you are going to have problems. This world is going to constantly throw things at you.

Then He says these words, "Be of good cheer, I have overcome the world." When I first read that my intuitive thought was, *Well, great for You, Jesus! - You may have overcome the world but I haven't!* It seems that the world just keeps on throwing stuff at me and it's not easy or fun.

The problem with the world throwing stuff at you is this; it affects you emotionally. You find that your emotions take you on a roller-coaster ride in life. There are periods of exhaustion and periods of depression as well as fear, worry and pain mixed in with the fulfillment and the joy. That is the way it is. To deal with this, some people suffocate their emotions so that they do not feel anything. Sometimes when people get hurt a lot in life they will cauterise their emotions because they cannot handle the pain. They do not want to suffer these negative feelings. However, when you do this you are repressing *all* your emotions. You cannot push down negative emotions and keep the positive ones alive. Some people think it's better not to be happy as long as you are not sad either. However your emotions can also be a source of great blessing in your life. To really enjoy something is a wonderful thing. The problem is that you pay for enjoyment with the capacity to be devastated.

So when Jesus says, "Be of good cheer. I have overcome the

world," my response was, *"That's great for You - but I haven't!"* My problem was that the world was still creating turmoil with my emotions. Jesus overcame the world but how does that pertain to me? How do *I* overcome the world?

I do not believe we can have an adequate and full answer to this until we have come to understand and receive the love of the Father. It is part of the development of Christianity that we are beginning to understand and have access to things that we have not had access to before. Prior to the Reformation, people didn't have access to a freedom from guilt until they had a revelation of sins forgiven. People back then lived without knowing how to get rid of that sense of guilt. Now that we understand Jesus' death on the cross, God's forgiveness and justification by faith, and the cleansing of our conscience by His blood, we can truly be free from guilt. It's a wonderful truth! Until you know that truth you cannot enter into the provision that it has secured.

THE SALVATION OF YOUR SOUL

The love of the Father is bringing us into an experience of Christianity that has not been seen before this time. So much happened when Jesus died on the cross. Let me headline some of these things that happened.

One of the things that happened when Jesus died on the cross was that He overcame the power of sin. When He died and shed His blood, that blood became available to us. He overcame sin Himself, and in doing so He made it accessible for all of us to overcome. He brought us into a freedom and an experience of sins forgiven.

When He died on the cross, Jesus overcame the power of Satan. Satan had a power and authority before Jesus' death that was completely lost to him afterwards.

By rising from the dead, Jesus overcame the power of death. Death no longer has the hold over us that it had before the death and resurrection of Jesus.

Jesus overcame many things which we have some understanding of, but one of the things that I didn't understand for many years was how He overcame *the world*. When He died on the cross, He overcame and broke the power of the world over Him, and He has opened the door for us to break the world's power over us. What did He mean by saying, "I have overcome the *world*?"

As a way of introducing what I want to say, let us look at it from another perspective. The Bible talks about three ways that we are saved. Scripture says: you *have* been saved, you *are being* saved, and you *will be* saved (Eph 2:5-8, 2 Tim 1:9, Tit 3:5; 1 Cor 1:18, 1 Cor 15:12, 2 Cor 2:15; Rom 8:23, 1 Thess 5:23). These speak of three different aspects of being saved. Firstly, when Jesus came into your life and your spirit connected with Him, you were saved. That was a 'done deal' for all eternity. Your salvation and your eternal destiny were secured, and cannot be taken from you. You *have been* saved. Your spirit has been saved.

Secondly, your *soul* is in the *process* of *being* saved. When Philippians 2:12 says, "...work out your own salvation with fear and trembling," it is talking about this process of the soul being saved. More of that in a minute.

Thirdly, in the area of our bodies we haven't even begun to be saved yet. There is a time coming when our bodies will be saved. Some of us are getting lines on our faces that didn't used to be there. Gravity seems to be winning the war and our chests are falling towards our stomachs! Your body is aging and will eventually die. But a day is coming when you will get a new body. I am hoping I will be super-fit without having to exercise. I am hoping I will be able to eat what I like and still be healthy! It is very clear that our bodies still have to be saved.

The area that I want to focus on, here, is the area in our lives that is *being* transformed - our souls. God is working to save our souls and to bring our soul-life into redemption. Your soul is made up of your mind, your will, and your emotions. When we define it in that way we can see how God is working in those three distinct areas. I believe that, up to now, we have seen Him working primarily in two of those areas - the mind and the will.

When you become a Christian, one of the things that you initially realise is that God wants to change the way you think. He is working to transform your thinking so that you will have the mind of Christ. In other words, until you start to think like God thinks. The work of the Spirit is to teach us *how* God thinks and reveal *what* He thinks so that we can begin to understand what it means to walk in agreement with Him. One of the really significant verses for me is Romans 3:4, "...let God be true but every man a liar." That very powerful verse tells us that God's priority in our lives is that we might embrace *His* truth. He wants us to see from His perspective and let go anything that we hold which is contrary to that. In other words, anything that is not the way that He thinks is a lie!

I remember one time I was talking to the Lord about speaking in tongues. I had been baptised in the Spirit and speaking in tongues for some time, but after a couple of years I found that speaking in tongues seemed pointless and boring to me. One day I read the Scripture in 1 Corinthians 14:4 where Paul says, "He who speaks with an unknown tongue edifies himself," which means 'to build yourself up' in your faith. When I read that verse I said to the Lord, "That's not working for me, Lord. I am speaking in tongues and finding it to be pretty boring!" As soon as I said that the verse was again imprinted firmly in my mind, "He who speaks in an unknown tongue *edifies* himself," and I repeated, "It's not working for me!" Again, the Lord repeated the verse back to me, to which I responded the same. Then, as clear as a bell, the Lord said to me, "*One of us* is lying."

Isn't He amazing? He deals so graciously with us. He has spoken to me in some of the kindest ways you could possibly imagine. So I said, "Lord, I'm sorry. Your Word is true. Even if I am not feeling it, it is still true." Then I began to speak in tongues believing I was being built up; then I experienced being encouraged in my heart. If you are contradicting what God is saying you will not experience what He has for you. You need to be transformed in your thinking and renewed in your mind. One of the big changes for Denise and I when we met Jack Winter was to believe that money could come to us supernaturally and not through the ways of capitalism. In other words, to get finance you don't have to have some profit-making system. Jack began to speak to us about faith for finances, about believing that God would provide supernaturally. I have seen money blowing in the wind down the street right into my outstretched hand! Believe it or not, money does grow on trees! We need our thinking reprogrammed to be like God's. We have an extremely wealthy

Father. If you are believing that money is always linked to capitalism then you will be locked into that system. Your faith will be in that system rather than in God.

God will reprogramme your thinking primarily through your feeding from the Bible. If you keep reading your Bible you will be transformed by the Spirit in your mind. Another way that God transforms your mind is to be in an environment where the Scriptures are preached. If you go to a church that mixes the philosophies of men with the Word of God it will not transform your mind to the mind of Christ. There is a battle for your mind.

There is also a battle for your will. When we come to Jesus our will is not submitted to Him. Our will wants its own way in all kinds of stuff. Our will can be completely untamed and can fluctuate a lot. We may have discipline in some areas but not in others. We can hype ourselves up to dedicate our lives to the will of God one moment and insist on doing our own thing the next. We can dedicate ourselves to God out of bravado rather than authentic faith and live in a pseudo consecration.

God wants to bring us to a place where we surrender our will to His will no matter who opposes us. There is a verse somewhere in Exodus that says, "Do not follow the crowd to do evil." In other words, if thousands of people are going to do something that you know to be wrong, be self-possessed enough to resist that. God is working in our will to align it with His will. This is a continual process throughout life as we face different choices. These are choices that are individual to you and they are crucial in determining the outcome of the battle for your will. There will be a struggle until you come to a place – and you will get there – where you genuinely love what God loves doing and there is no battle any more.

Ex 23:2

There is only a battle in your will when God wants you to do something that you really do not want to do. That is where the battle is. When I was a young Christian the major battle for me concerned my life as a professional hunter. I knew that the Lord was speaking to me about laying it down completely. It took a while for that to sink in but there came a day when the issue came to a head and reached a crisis point. One night we had visitors and I was so challenged in my heart that I couldn't act normally. I excused myself and went to the bedroom and knelt by the bed, weeping. I was faced with the reality of what God wanted me to do and I couldn't do it. What He wanted me to do was to burn my journals and photographs, get rid of my rifle and destroy the trophy antlers that I had accumulated in years of hunting.

I was trapped in the struggle of wanting to do God's will but also wanting to hold onto my possessions. Those things were the trappings of my whole identity. Some people go hunting but I was *a hunter*. There's a big difference between the two. Suddenly the presence of the Lord came into the room and I was filled with joy in His presence. My tears turned to laughter and the joy of the Lord filled me. When it reached a peak the Lord spoke to me and said, "Do it now while you have the strength!" Immediately and without hesitation I went to the wardrobe and took down my journals and photographs in which I had chronicled all my times in the mountains. My whole life was in those books. I took them and went straight to the living room, tore them in pieces, and knelt down and put them on the fire. As they burned I was filled with joy again. I didn't realise how much these things were binding me. I was bound in an identity as a hunter and He freed me into an identity as a man of God. The Lord will only challenge you to get rid of that which hinders you. He will never take anything away that is a blessing to you. He wants to get rid of the things that get in the way of blessing you more. That is an example of where I surrendered my will to God's will for my life. If you respond to Him in those moments of choice, you will prevail in the battle of your will.

THE BATTLE FOR YOUR EMOTIONS

The battle for our mind and the battle for our will are very familiar battles for us all. The other component of our souls is our emotions and there is also a battle for this area. However, I do not believe we have had the key to win this battle - *until we have come to know and experience the love of the Father.* Most Christians believe that you have to renew your mind and surrender your will and simply discipline yourself in your emotional life. In other words, believe the truth resolutely enough that your emotions will be how they are meant to be; that by believing strongly enough at a mind level you will have peace in your heart, patience, kindness, long-suffering and the rest. We so often say things like, "I need more patience," but let me tell you - you cannot get it! There is no provision for patience. Patience is a byproduct of something else. It is the same with joy, kindness and gentleness. They are fruits. They come from something else. The fruit of the Spirit is emotion-driven and expressed. The fruit of the Spirit is the product of a greater ruling emotion.

There is a battle going on for our emotions. The reality of it is that our spiritual lives are thrown around by our emotions. Wouldn't you like to get off that rollercoaster of your emotions? Wouldn't you like to be in a place where you are not dictated to by your emotions?

I understand this battle well. It has been very real for me

personally. I have found that trying to stifle and control the emotions can work for a while, but there will come a day when the stuff will hit the proverbial fan. A situation will arise and overwhelm you and the dam will break. You will find that you have no control over your emotions. I can tell you this, however: the Lord *has* provision.

This verse, where Jesus says, "Be of good cheer I have overcome the world," what does that mean? How did Jesus overcome the world? This is talking about the battle for *His* emotions. Satan wanted control over Him, but Jesus resisted Satan. Sin had no control over Him, but He also stopped *the world* from having any influence whatsoever on Him - He overcame it.

When we look at Jesus' life the reality is this. In the last days before He was crucified, Satan threw at Him everything that the world could possibly throw at one individual. Jesus lived the years of His ministry having overcome the Tempter at the beginning but then He said, "The ruler of this world is coming and he has nothing in Me." (John 14:30) Jesus knew that the one who was the ruling power behind the world system was returning to try to influence Him. Jesus knew that Satan would unleash everything he could muster in the entire world to divert Him from fulfilling the will of the Father. In Ephesians 2, Satan is called "...the prince of the power of the air, the spirit that is now at work in the sons of disobedience." Another scripture (Rev 12:9) calls Satan, "the deceiver of the whole world." He is the spirit of the world, influencing the way it functions. Satan is engineering the world to walk down his path.

When we lived in the world, we were totally defenceless against it. Until you are born again there is no freedom from the world. In fact, you may not even believe that Satan exists until you are born again; and then you realise that you have been saved from his clutches and you are beginning to be free of him.

Jesus knew that the time was imminent when Satan would unleash his final attack. This attack commenced in the garden of Gethsemane. In that garden Jesus cried out to His Father, "...if it is possible let this cup pass from Me." In other words, "If there is any way that I don't have to experience what is coming – let it pass from Me." Then, He surrendered Himself to the will of the Father. The 'cup' that He asked to be spared from was *not* the cup of crucifixion. The 'cup' that He was talking about was the cup of sin-bearing. As the Lamb of God, all sins past, present and future of the human race were put upon Him.

I cannot imagine what it was like for Jesus to have the sins of all time to be imparted to Him. The accumulated guilt and hopelessness of the sins of all time descended upon Jesus emotionally right there in the garden of Gethsemane. The shock and trauma of this made Him sweat drops of blood. Sin puts a terrible burden on the individual. When I was saved I felt such relief when the burden of sin lifted off. Back then I didn't realise where it had gone. It went onto Jesus! It is an unimaginable thing. The Bible says that Jesus *became* sin. In other words, He experienced the consequences of all of the sin of the whole world throughout all time. The Holy One became sin. The horror of that happened at Gethsemane. Immediately the sense of His Father's presence was lost to Him. He is taken and beaten. You may have seen the film *The Passion of the Christ* but that doesn't show the half of it. He was beaten with rods, which would have smashed His face beyond recognition. Then the Romans whipped Him. The Roman whipping was much more severe than any other. They used a whip with hooks, blades and pieces of bone interlaced into it. This separated flesh from bone and if a person didn't die from it they were certainly crippled for life.

One of the greatest sufferings for Jesus was to hear the leaders of Israel cry out repeatedly, "Crucify Him! Crucify Him!" These were the leaders of Israel, which He loved as a bride. The truth is, Satan threw everything he possibly could to make the Son of God lose it emotionally. But Jesus hung there on the cross, more concerned with others than Himself. He showed concern for His mother and John. He showed concern for the thief beside Him. He prayed for those who crucified Him. In the midst of it all He still continued to do the perfect will of the Father and never 'lost it' emotionally. Hebrews 12:2 tells us, "...who for the joy that was set before Him endured the cross, despising the shame." His responses were perfect. He never got angry, never felt self-pity, never gave up on His purpose. He continued to do everything perfectly under the most extreme emotional torment that any human has ever faced. He overcame all that the world used to destroy Him by not being affected by it emotionally and descending into carnal responses.

HOW JESUS OVERCAME THE WORLD

The question that occurs to me is – how did He do it? How did He manage to keep His equilibrium? I believe that Jesus was able to go through all of that because He had a history with the Father. He was absolutely stable and secure in His experience of the Father loving Him. He was unwaveringly convinced that He was loved by all the Love in the universe. And *that* love gave Him the stability to endure all that He endured.

The New Covenant *is* the love of God poured into our hearts. As His love continues to pour into your heart and accumulate in your heart, finally what will happen is that His love for you will become more real than the problems this world throws at you. The emotional reality of the Father loving you will finally eclipse the emotional turmoil of your life. His love for you will become the supreme reality. You will be so influenced by His love for you that it will produce joy automatically even in the face of the problematic turmoil of life in this world.

I remember a lady who was at one of our meetings. She had crashed her car on the way to the meeting and was very nervous about breaking the news to her husband. The love of the Father hit her during the meeting and as she began laughing her anxiety washed away. The love of the Father became increasingly real to her and filled her with joy. The love of the Father poured into your heart will automatically cause your emotions to change too!

His love poured into your heart is going to make you joyful even when bad things seem to be happening around you. You will never be rid of the tribulations of the world. They are going to keep happening all of your life but His love will eclipse the *effect* of them. Most of us try to fix our internal issues by trying to address external problems. We think that if we get everything peaceful on the outside then we will be at peace in our hearts. If I can get everything happy around me then *I* can be happy. If I can get everything nice on the outside, then I will feel nice on the inside. If everything is structured in order to minimise the frustrations, then I won't get frustrated internally. If I can stop others being such frustrating people then I can be free of frustration. We try to get the externals of life fixed so that we can be at peace. That is what arguments and fights are really about.

The disharmony and aggression between people is all down to – if I can just get *you* to do it right then I will be happy.

The point is – the other person will *always* do it wrong. The people around you will *never* do it the way you want it to be done. They will always do things that are going to frustrate you. In this world you *will* have tribulation. It's never going to be any different. That is the best news you can ever have! Why? Because then you can start to deal with it. If you believe it is going to change then you will be waiting for the day it will all be better. You will be waiting for the day that your husband or wife is going to change or the day when your children will finally get the message. You will be waiting for the day when you get a new boss or a new job, or when you finally get the car you really want. You will always be waiting for the day to arrive when everything is perfect.

Can you grasp and understand that, no matter what does actually change for the better, something else bad will come? In this world you *will* have tribulation. It's going to keep on, and it will be the same for the rest of your life. However, if the fire is going on the inside, you won't feel the cold on the outside. If you have peace on the *inside* the turmoil outside won't affect you. If you have inner joy, your circumstances may shift and change, but *nothing* will move that joy in your heart. If you are filled with the substance of His love on the inside, then the problems of life won't shake you.

Overcoming the world is not the same as fixing it. A lot of people want to fix the world. They want to fix the political system. They want to get the right party into government, or the right president into power. Many Christians are trying to fix the world. We think if we can finally fix the world around us then we can all be at peace. The truth is - it's never going to happen.

THE VICTORY THAT OVERCOMES THE WORLD

No matter what storms are raging on the outside you can be at peace. God has provided a way. What is that way? It is the love of the Father being poured into your heart. As His love pours into your heart you will come to know beyond all shadow of doubt that you are absolutely loved by Almighty God who is your Father. I love to remind myself that my Father just happens to be Almighty God!

When you become completely convinced that Almighty God loves you as a father then, no matter what happens around you, you will see that it really isn't a big deal. The problems of the world? No big deal! His love in your heart will bring you to a place of peace where, even if the world is at war, you will be at peace on the inside. I am learning that it is a good place to be. I'm in a much different place than I used to be. The most significant sign of this change for me is that my own family has noticed it. The difference in me has shocked them. I am very different to the person I once was.

It is about becoming like Jesus. He lived in a world more evil than today's world. He lived in an enslaved nation and in the most poverty-stricken part of it. But He grew up in the love of His Father and in inner peace, joy, love and contentment. He lived above the world's turmoil and so can deliver us from it too!

This change in my emotions wasn't when I understood that God loved me as a father. It wasn't when He healed my heart of a lot of wounds. This overcoming in my emotional life has only happened as I have learned to *experience* Him loving me in a *more continuous* way. Day by day experiencing His loving. All kinds of things still arise which threaten to affect me emotionally. Let me tell you one story of what I have experienced.

Some years ago I was in Ukraine. I had travelled far out into the countryside, about a twelve-hour train ride from Kiev. It was a very remote place and I was to spend the weekend there ministering. I was supposed to be back in Kiev to catch the plane out on Monday morning, so I needed to catch the train on Sunday night. When I arrived the pastor told me that he had not been able to secure a return ticket for me. I asked him what we should do about it and his reply was that all the tickets had been sold. I decided to trust God for getting me back to Kiev.

We had two days of ministry in this remote place. Thirty minutes after getting there I baptised twenty people in a pond. Then the pastor left me with some people and he disappeared. I spent about five hours with these people who couldn't speak a word of English. I didn't know what was happening and whether or not I could trust this man who had deserted me there. Finally the pastor came and took me to where I was staying for the night. The following morning I spoke at a church and then we had to dash to another church where I was due to speak. We drove at speed along some very bumpy roads. At the next church, just as I was about to get up to speak, I opened my bag and was horrified to discover that a bottle of water had leaked all over my laptop computer. I turned it on but all that happened was a message on the screen, "Operating system not found." I quickly closed it but I believed that everything on the computer was lost - all my work, all my email contacts, everything was lost. Then I had to get up and preach about the love of the Father.

Somehow I got through that meeting. Most of the eight hundred people in the congregation wanted us to pray for them afterwards. We prayed for as many as we could until we could stay no longer. We rushed to the train station where the pastor ran along the platform trying to find someone to somehow get a ticket, which he did. I got on the overnight train to Kiev and struggled to sleep through the night on a narrow bunk in a stinking carriage crammed full of people. Finally we got to the railway station in Kiev with ninety minutes to spare in which to get to the airport. I was flying to Frankfurt and then to Munich. As we pulled into the airport the car driver asked me, "Have you got your departure form?" to which I replied, "What departure form?" I didn't recall receiving one - in fact they didn't even stamp my passport when I entered the country.

Things were going from bad to worse. I needed a departure form to leave the country. After much confusion and negotiation at the airport they let me through without a departure card. Arriving in the packed departure lounge there was no movement to board the plane. We waited for hours and then they announced that the flight was cancelled. What was more they announced that all tickets would have to be reissued. The desk for reissuing fresh tickets was down a very narrow corridor. The entire crowd of people on our flight began to queue up with their luggage down this tight space. It was chaos. Tempers were fraying. When I eventually reached the counter I was issued with a ticket and went to queue for the bus that was to take us to the hotel provided by the airline because of the cancelled flight. Somehow I couldn't shake off a feeling of uneasiness about the replacement ticket that had been issued. I approached one of the staff and asked her to look at the ticket. All she could do was shake her head. My ticket was wrong!

I had to trust her to get me the correct ticket so I took a deep breath and handed my passport to her. Would I ever see it again? Would I ever leave this country? Thankfully she procured me a good ticket and I was able to fly to Frankfurt the next morning, and then to Munich. When I arrived there I stood waiting at the carousel for my luggage. I waited in vain. My luggage had gone missing! Remember that my laptop wasn't working so I couldn't tell anyone that I was running a day late. There was no one there to meet me at the airport. I decided to book into a hotel in Munich just to get some sleep. I was kept awake all night with people constantly tramping up and down the corridor outside my room. When I got up the next morning my luggage had been found and was waiting for me. I decided that I would go to the train station to get a train to the house where I was staying. As I stepped out onto the street I quickly found out that the hotel where I had spent the night was right in the middle of the red light district! I needed to get out of there quickly!

I caught the train to the town of my final destination but it was diverted because of work being done on the track. When I eventually arrived at my host's house there was no one at home but the neighbours had a key to let me in. I walked into the house and closed the door behind me. I put my laptop in the airing cupboard and it dried out. The ordeal was finally over.

In this world everything that can go wrong will go wrong. There *is* a battle for your emotions. This world will throw everything it can at you. The battle is won by opening your heart to the love of the Father. As His love goes deeper and deeper into your heart, you will be more and more convinced of His love for you. As you experience that love it accumulates inside you and it *will change* your emotions. You will begin to have peace when everything is going wrong. His love for you becomes more substantial and important than the other things. You will be concerned with other people's problems even when yours are bigger. Filled with His love you won't be worried about your problems anymore.

His love poured into your heart is the *only* provision for your emotional stability. Emotional stability doesn't come through trying to convince yourself of some biblical truth. The reality is – He is loving you right now. The adventure is – to learn how to experience that love more and more. That is the victory that overcomes the world.

CHAPTER SEVEN

~

Abiding in Love

As I said in my introduction, I have written this book with one main aim. It is for those who will be the communicators of the Gospel in future generations. I truly believe that the Gospel as God intends it to be preached is the good news that we can know and experience the love of the Father. That is the Tree of Life. That is the Good News.

My observation of the Church throughout history, however, is that it has known very little of love. Throughout the forty or more years that I have been a Christian, I have observed that we in the Body of Christ have really struggled to love one another. Leaders within churches have rivalries. Denominations are at odds with one another. There are jealousies among many believers. Splits and factions have been rife within the Body of Christ. Love is talked about a lot but the living actuality of it is all too often absent. There seems to be a yawning chasm between this and what the New Testament speaks about as a vibrant reality.

Many statements in the New Testament are perplexing. Even Peter admitted that he found some of Paul's statements difficult to understand. Some of John's statements too, are very difficult to receive *until* you come to an understanding of what he is talking about. I want to look in some detail at John's epistles, specifically 1 John 4. This passage has statements in it that I have struggled with, statements such as verse 8, which says, *"He who does not love does not know God."* We confuse the biblical concept of love with our own human capacity to love. Of course, when the Scriptures talk about love here they are talking about the love *of God*. And that love is a very specific kind of love.

Many are familiar with the Greek definitions of love - *phileo, eros, storge* and *agape*. These words are used to describe love in its different expressions. We have tried to understand the Scriptures by defining the word that is used in a particular text. We can look at the original language and find out what word is used. We have resources to hand such as the *Greek-English Lexicon* or *Vine's Expository Dictionary*. These resources give us a handle on what the word actually means and they are very helpful. However, in reality, we will never understand what the Bible means *except* by revelation. Unless the *substance* of love actually touches us, unless something of God actually opens our eyes, we will not really enter into what the Scriptures are intending to teach us. Study can help us to understand many things but even that will fall far short of what happens when the Holy Spirit opens our spiritual eyes to really see something.

I remember having a discussion with a man years ago and I asked him, "Do you believe that the Bible can be completely understood through study alone?" His reply was an unequivocal "Yes!" to which I responded, "That is the difference between you and me because I believe that the Bible can only be understood through revelation!" The Bible was penned by persons *in* personal revival, it was written *about* revival and it is only properly understood *in revival*. It is only properly understood in the context of the manifest presence of God in our lives. When I use the word 'revival', I am not referring to the phenomenon of outpoured revival. Rather, I am talking about a heart-revival in which the heart of the individual is opened to the stirrings of the Holy Spirit. The Spirit of God living in you will teach you what is written in the Scriptures. 1 John 2:27 talks of an "anointing that abides" - that anointing is the Spirit of God within us, and it is only the Spirit of God who can really interpret the word of God to us. Our own study will never be able to achieve that.

As we look at this fourth chapter of John's first epistle, there is one problem that we are immediately faced with, which affects our understanding of the chapter. The problem is this: John didn't write in logical sequence. In actual fact, the Bible, in its entirety, is not written logically and sequentially. The major subject headings and the core statements are hidden within the body of the text. They are not written in bold type and underlined so that the casual reader can easily grasp them. The Holy Spirit needs to highlight the important statements to our spirits. We do not, for example, have Point 1 followed by Point 2 with subheadings underneath. If the Bible was written like that, it would be so much easier to grasp what is written in it. The Bible is not accessible to someone who approaches God in a casual and offhand manner. It is opened by the Spirit to the heart.

I want to highlight a couple of statements made by the apostle John, which, I believe, are the major headings of this epistle. The first major statement appears in verse 19. The whole chapter and its content hinges on what this verse says. Verse 19 states, "We love Him because He first loved us." This verse unequivocally declares that we cannot come into anything of love apart from knowing the reality, the experience of God first loving us. That is the crux of it.

GOD, THE SOURCE OF LOVE

God is the original Lover. He loved you before you ever loved Him. All of the energy, substance and reality of knowing God's love for others originates in our experiencing Him loving us. We love because He *first* loved us. He didn't just love us as a one-off historical event. He is continually loving us. We have a tendency to confine statements such as, "For God so loved the world.." to the past, to Jesus' day. We take as a purely historical reality that He sent His Son to die for us. The question, however, is; does God still love the world today? We have no problem accepting that He loved the world in the first century, when Jesus was born as a babe in Bethlehem's manger, but does God love the world in *this* day? Does He, for example, love the Muslims today? Does He *still* love criminals and prostitutes twenty centuries later? Sometimes I feel uneasy inside myself when I think of this. We can handle the fact that God loved the world in the past. That is a relatively easy concept to grasp because the harsh and messy reality of that is removed from us. *But does He love the world in the same way now?* In our everyday world, with the things that we experience, we struggle to love the people who do things that we do not love. But is it still true that God loves *this* world that we live in and everyone in it, *now*?

It would be very interesting to know what the world of Jesus' day was actually like. What kinds of atrocities were being perpetrated across the globe when Jesus walked this earth? There were certainly atrocities such as slavery being committed. Slavery continues to be one the great evils of the world, but it was a greater evil in those days, a fundamental and widespread part of the social fabric. What was happening in China, for example, in the years when Jesus walked upon the earth? What was transpiring in some remote kingdom unknown to writers of that time? The world of Jesus' day was not a better world and therefore easier for God to love. His love didn't flow more freely in the first century than it does in the twenty-first century. He loves the world continuously! We tend to lose connection with that reality. We find it difficult to comprehend that God loves every person in the world right now.

John says that we love Him *because* He first loved us. This statement is the axis on which this whole chapter turns. This is, in my view, the true heading which the Spirit underlines. It is *the* statement that He has penned in bold type. It defines all the other statements about love.

LOVE IS THE MARK OF TRUE CHRISTIANITY

If we read back from verse 19 there is another statement in verse 7 which I wish to highlight. I used to have a great deal of difficulty with this verse. This letter was written by the apostle John to a Christianity that was already being greatly affected by wrong influences. One of the major heresies in that era was Gnosticism and it was infiltrating the early Christian community in a significant way. John wrote this letter to counter that influence, and he counters it by describing what true Christianity actually is. I find this very interesting. Why? Because a huge part of this letter is talking about love. In this letter, John declares unambiguously that love is really the mark of true Christianity. Verse 7 of chapter 4 states, "Beloved, let us love one another for love is of God and everyone who loves is born of God." I remember reading that statement and having real difficulty with it.

I had an aunt who was an extremely loving person, but to my knowledge she wasn't a Christian. Her many nieces and nephews would really enjoy staying at her house because she was such a wonderful woman but she never professed to be 'born again.' Yet, this scripture says that everyone who loves is born of God! How does that fit? Maybe my aunt was a secret Christian? So what is this statement in John talking about?

The issue here is how the word 'love' is defined. This is not talking about a person who loves on a merely human scale or who has the natural aptitude to be a loving person. This statement in John is talking about a person who has received *the love of God.* The truth is – if you have received the love of God then you *will* love. You cannot do otherwise.

"Everyone who loves is born of God and knows God." Then it continues: "He who does not love does not know God for God is love." These statements have been a huge problem for me. I wonder how many others have also struggled with these statements. He who does not love does not know God! Why has that caused me much consternation over the years? Because I believed that the one who does not love is not *born again.*

You see, I equated 'knowing God' with being 'born again.' When you are born again, that is when you come to know the Lord and God in Jesus becomes real to you? Right? So in my thinking this verse was calling into question the reality of being born again. I was absolutely sure that I was genuinely born again but there were many people who I didn't love. I really struggled in my heart to love some people. The truth is that I came to the Lord with no trust of anyone in my heart at all. I fundamentally trusted no one in the world. I had rejected the world. When I was a young man I just wanted to live as a hermit in the mountains. The reason for that was because I believed that people would always hurt me and cause me pain and rejection. I thought that if I could live without people I could also live without pain. I went on to become a deer culler, living alone in the hills. I would shoot deer, carry them out of the hills into the town, sell them, return to the hills before nightfall and be alone again. From the age of ten I had a consuming desire to be a hermit. The problem, which I discovered before too long, was that I couldn't cope with the loneliness.

I have since thought that I must have been pretty arrogant to reject the entire human race as having any real validity! I have often commented to Denise that I felt as if I was sitting outside the human race observing it through a window. I have often said to her over the years, "Am I really a human being?" I felt so separated from what I perceived everyone else to be like.

When it comes to this statement from verse 7 - "He who does not love does not know God" - where do you go with that when you know for sure that you are born again but you do not have love for people in your heart? I think we can all identify with that to a greater or lesser degree. The Lord has done a lot of work in my heart over the years and I have gained some ground. What this verse is *not* saying is - if you do not love then you are not born again. What it *is* saying is - if you do not love you are not connected to the love of the Father. That is the true meaning - if you do not love, you are not knowing Him intimately in that moment!

When you are in intimate connection with the love of the Father, you cannot do anything *but* love. It is simply a matter of cause and effect. Being intimately connected with the love of the Father will automatically cause you to love others out of that selfsame love. It is not an issue of being 'born again' it is about having the reality of that love in your heart. If you do not have love in your heart, you are not knowing Him in that moment. You are not at that time intimately connected with God loving you with *His* love.

Let me pose a couple of questions:

Are you and I, at this moment, *in* the love of the Father?

Are you and I experiencing Him loving us at this time right now?

One of the tests of that is this: If you are not loving others then you are not in connection with the Father's love. It is as simple as that.

No matter what we claim or what our lips say - if the love of God is not coming out of us, then the love of God is not coming *into* us. We love because He first loved us. The whole point is Him loving us. Many of us feel guilty when we don't love the other person enough. We often feel a need to repent for the lack of love towards that person. Let me say this. I'm not convinced that repentance is really the focus here. I believe that the real issue is in recognising that you have slipped out of intimacy with the Father - because when you are in a place of intimacy with Him, that love for others will be resident within your heart. We often associate repentance with emotions such as sorrow or remorse over not fulfilling what God requires of us. Then we feel the need to feel guilty, to be sorry about it, and ask God's forgiveness. That is very much our understanding of what repentance is. Yet repentance actually means 'to turn around.' It doesn't have any sense of sorrow, sadness or remorse attached to it. The original meaning of the Greek word *metanoia* is 'to turn around and face in the opposite direction.' It simply conveys the thought of changing one's mind. When we repent, we simply turn back to God and to His love, to receiving His love.

Many people have shed a lot of tears when they have asked God's forgiveness for their sins. The remorse and sorrow associated with that is an individual matter for each person. Some people feel tremendous remorse over their sinful lives and that is appropriate and good – but it does not, in itself, constitute repentance. Repentance with emotion is no more valid than repentance without emotion. Many people want to see the penitent sinner weeping before God but that is not actually a requirement of repentance. It might be necessary for the release of the emotions but it is not specifically an ingredient of repentance. Repentance is the product of that remorse and sorrow. Some people can be extremely sorry for their sins yet not change anything so the sorrow in itself is not repentance. What is required in repentance is to turn around, change your mind and go in the opposite direction. When we recognise that we are lacking in love for people it is not a matter of feeling bad – and then resolving to do better in the future. You will not do better in the future – you cannot! It is motivated by Him! When there are things in us that are not loving, we need to recognise that it is as a result of our lack of receiving His love in our lives.

LOVE IS A SUBSTANCE

We need to realise that the substance of His love is the whole point of Christianity. Christianity is not about *the message* of His love or about the truth that He loves us. It is about receiving *love* itself. Merely understanding the concept of God's love for you will not change you. What will change you is the actual love of God being poured into your heart. It is not the adherence to the theological truth of it that will heal you and set you free. It is the *substance* of the Father's love that will do this. Living in the continuous experience of being loved by the Father is what sonship is. We need to be really focused on this issue. We are carrying *the love* of the Father to the world. We are not carrying *the message* of the love of the Father to the world. We are carrying *His love*. This is one of the reasons why I have been uncomfortable with the term, "The message of the Father's love." Those who use this term haven't really got the point. It is the substance of His love that we take - not the message of it. In this chapter, John is talking about the *actual substance* of the Father's love.

I have begun to realise that the substance of God's love is actually the same substance as God Himself. It is His life. It is not so much that He loves you; it is the fact that when He comes you are loved - because He *is* love. The substance of love *is* His presence. When we began to realise that love is a substance, it was the doorway into this continually unfolding revelation.

Let me give an example here of what I mean when I say that love is a substance. When I was a young guy, I lived in a small town in New Zealand. It was a rural town; the population mainly consisted of farmers and their families. The men were men of the land, very hardworking and weather-beaten with calloused hands. I never heard a man sing until I was twelve years of age. Where I come from, men don't sing!

I remember attending a gathering in the community hall when I was about fourteen years old. I don't remember what the purpose of the gathering was but I do remember there were approximately thirty people there, which seemed like a large crowd at the time. In those days I was a very depressed and emotionally wounded young man. People used to say that I was moody but they had no idea what was going on inside me. I was completely lost and out of my depth. I remember a man said to me once, "You shouldn't be so sad - these are the best years of your life!" I looked at him and thought, *"Do you mean to say - it gets worse?"* Not long after that I took a rifle, loaded it with a single bullet and sat by a tree in the dark - with the loaded rifle - thinking that if life got any worse then I didn't want to stick around to see that. That was what my life was like then.

When I was at this gathering of people in the community hall, I recall something happening in the room. Whatever it was that happened, it caused everyone in the room to burst out laughing. They all laughed except me and, as I discovered later, someone else. As I was standing by the wall observing everybody laughing and feeling totally detached from it, suddenly I caught the eye of a man across the room who was looking straight at me. It was Ross, the father of my best friends who were identical twins. Ross was a high-country shepherd in the South Island of New Zealand. During the shearing season he would shear sheep all day from dawn until nightfall. In my opinion, shearing sheep is one of the hardest jobs a man can do. Working for long hours in the heat of a summer's day in a shed without air circulation, constantly bent over, covered in lanolin oil. It is extremely arduous work.

187

Ross told me that he would often go to the bathroom during a day's shearing and cough up blood from the sheer exertion. He would toil from dawn to dusk seven days a week to provide for his family.

Being only fourteen at the time of this meeting in the community hall, I did not know my friends' father as Ross, I knew him as 'Mr. Smith'. When the laughter broke out across the room, I caught his eye. I can still visualise his weather-beaten face and his eyes that would squint to block out the intense glare of the New Zealand sun. He looked at me across that room, *and raised one eyebrow*. And in that moment I felt his love for me. I didn't know that he loved me until that moment but his love for me was transmitted across that room and I knew, without a shadow of a doubt, that he loved me. I felt the substance of his fatherly love. It was a hugely significant moment in my life, one that I have never forgotten. Ross was a quiet man but he was a man that was as strong as steel. I later spent a lot of time with him and his twin boys trapping, fishing and hunting together. He was a significant person in my young life. When he looked at me across the crowded room that evening and simply raised one eyebrow, I learned something that I have never forgotten. I learned that love *is a substance*.

A person can say the words "I love you" but they mean nothing if there is no substance of love conveyed. Another person, however, can merely raise an eyebrow and you can get filled with love - because love is a substance.

When we read the statement, "We love because He first loved us" it is as if God Himself was across the room, catching your eye and raising one eyebrow. In some inexplicable way you experience Him loving you. In that moment, when that happens, you *will* love the world. You cannot fail to do so when you are being loved by Him. The statement, "We love because He first loved us" is not talking about salvation. It is not talking about the 'born again' experience. It is talking about the living connection with God the Father. God the Father is the source of all love. Jesus loves us – true! But He loves us with the love of His Father. Paul, in the epistle to the Romans (8:39) tells us very clearly that, "...nothing can separate us from the love of God, which is in Christ Jesus our Lord." The love of God the Father is in Jesus. In the final verse of John 17, Jesus prays to His Father using these amazing words:

> *"...and I have declared to them Your name and will declare it...that the love with which You have loved Me may be in them, and I in them."*

That the love with which the Father loves the Son *may be in us*. In other words, Jesus prayed that we would experience the Father loving us as He, the Son, experienced the Father loving Him. That is an utterly amazing thing to pray – that we would know the selfsame love that the Father has for His beloved Son.

MAKE LOVE YOUR GREAT AIM

Here is the good news! The whole gospel is wrapped up in this one thing. Jesus died on the cross to get rid of all the stuff that gets in the way so that you and I would come into the love of the Father! We can know that in concept more than we can know it in our experience. I want to seriously put it to you now as you are reading this book – continually seek to experience that love! Continuously reach out to know the reality of His love for you. I like how the Revised Standard Version puts the first verse of 1 Corinthians 14. It says, *"Make love your great aim."* This doesn't mean that you should make becoming a loving person your aim in life. It means to make the love that is in the Father your greatest aim in life - for God *is* love.

What I have discovered is this - in love you cannot be offended. When you are living in the love of God, it is just impossible to be offended. Someone told me recently of how hurt they were at comments made to them by another person. My response to them was, "What is in you that is able to be hurt?" - because, when there is love in you, you cannot be hurt or offended. Love overwhelms all of the offence. Love says, "I do not care what you do to me because I love you." When Jesus was hanging on the cross He was loving those who had hammered the nails into His hands and feet. He wanted them to be forgiven. His desire was that they should be free. Love is impervious to the pain of rejection. You can only be rejected when you are outside of love. You can only be hurt outside the circumference of love. To be in the place of love is an incredibly strong place to be. In fact, it is the only place that is truly free.

What happens when you are not in the love of God? You are vulnerable because your emotions can be played with. People will mess with your emotions. They will manipulate you. They will do things, wittingly or unwittingly, that will cause your life to be on an emotional rollercoaster. In every situation you find yourself in, you will be subject to the ups and downs of your emotions according to how you perceive others treat you. Something they may say, or how they look at you will cause you to be tossed about on the sea of emotions. In love there is no place to feel rejected if someone doesn't like you. You are in an unassailable place of security in the love of the Father. How can the rejection or the desire of someone to hurt us possibly affect us when we are wrapped in the reality and totality of the loving of the Creator of all things?

When we do feel hurt and rejected we need to realise that it is because we are not vitally connected to His love in that moment. That is the real issue; it is not about you failing to please God or being a good enough Christian. As you connect in your heart to His love and the reality that He is loving you, you *will* become a loving person.

Years ago, when Denise and I were young Christians, we (along with another couple) planted a church in the little town where we lived. We had lived there since we got married. We had been travelling fifty or so kilometres to church every week so we decided to plant a little church right in the town where we lived, so that we could bring the spiritual life that we had been experiencing to that town. We hired a hall and began to hold services there and, after a while, we had gathered about sixty people. We baptised the new converts in a little creek and they formed the nucleus of the fellowship into which we poured everything that was in us.

After we had being doing this for a year or so, the elders of another church in the town invited Peter and I to attend their meeting one night. We were overjoyed when we received their invitation. We thought that they wanted to encourage us and really promote unity within the Body of Christ in our local town. So we went along in our naiveté to the elders' meeting. When we arrived they welcomed us with cups of tea and biscuits. After some friendly chat we went in to the adjoining room and sat down for the meeting. For the next three hours they bombarded us with warnings that we should immediately stop what we were doing in our new church. They told us that we were rebellious and that we were in contravention of God's will for the town. The upshot of it was that they wanted us to join their church and bring the life of the Spirit that we were experiencing to *their* young people.

We came out of that meeting feeling really battered and bruised by what they had said. Peter drove me back to our house, which was out in the countryside, entirely surrounded, by fields, with no other houses nearby. When we arrived at the house, Peter turned to me and said, "Before you go into the house, let's take a moment to pray." We didn't get a chance to say anything, because the moment we turned towards each other to pray, the love of God suddenly came and filled the car. The love of God absolutely and utterly filled the car and filled us. We could do nothing else but hold onto each other for what seemed like a long time as the presence of God filled us. We just embraced each other and wept. We were stunned and overwhelmed by the intensity of His presence.

Finally, I got out of the car and Peter drove home. As I walked towards the house I noticed that the bedroom light was on. Denise was waiting up for me. I went immediately to the bedroom and she was sitting up in bed. Her first words were, "Well, how did the meeting go?" but all I could say was, "They were such wonderful guys - amazing men!" I couldn't get any other words out of my mouth apart from saying how wonderful the elders of the other church were. In my mind I was thinking, *"I know that is not the whole truth about what happened in the meeting this evening,"* but I couldn't recall a single thing that had been said that night.

You see, love cannot be offended. When the love of God filled us as we sat in the car, I found that I couldn't remember any of the harsh words against Peter or me. Love cannot be offended nor does it even remember the sins against it. That is why God can say in Hebrews 8:12, "...I will remember their sins no more." After hearing me say how wonderful these elders were, Denise thought that we would from now on be attending the other church! We didn't.

I have discovered something about love. Love changes you into everything that God has ever intended for you to be. Love will turn you into being a mature Christian. Love will cause you to turn the other cheek without even knowing it because the other person will be more important to you than preserving your own cheek! It is not that we grit our teeth and reluctantly think, *I must turn the other cheek.* Love cares for the other person rather than trying to maintain our own self-respect.

Years ago, when I was lecturing at Bible School, there was a young Maori guy living on the campus there who was very angry and we were trying to help him. One day I had talked to him about the Lord. Later that evening, after the communal meal, I went up to the counter in the dining room to get a cup of tea. As I was standing there he arrived at the counter and suddenly picked up the full teapot (and it was a large teapot) and threw the hot tea into my face. The tea was almost boiling and he threw it full in my face. It went under my eyelids, into my mouth and up my nostrils. To this day it confounds me why I did not suffer serious burns. I remember just looking at him and all I could see in front of me was a young guy who was trapped in his own inner pain and anger. There was nothing in me that was concerned about my own wellbeing. My only concern was for this poor guy who was motivated to hurl the contents of a boiling teapot into my face. I was concerned for the terrible situation he had been in. When you are connected to love, that selfsame love compels you to love without any conditions. The connection in intimacy to the love of God is what generates love for others. When you realise that you have insufficient love just come to God for the infilling of that love.

LOVE IS THE ENERGY THAT
MAKES YOU A CHRISTIAN

The last verse in this fourth chapter of John that I wish to comment on is verse 20. This is another verse that I have really struggled with in my Christian life. It says:

If someone says, "I love God," and hates his brother, he is a liar; for he who does not love his brother whom he has seen, how can he love God whom he has not seen?

This is one of those statements in Scripture that really needs to be read in reverse. Because, if you can receive the love of God whom you cannot see, you will then have love for your brother whom you can see. This links so strongly with the verse that says, "We love because He first loved us." You see, if you say that you love God but hate your brother, this means, according to John, that you are liar. Why? Because you need to be receiving the love of God to really love your brother. It doesn't mean that you are not a Christian. It doesn't infer that you are not 'born again.' It means that you are not living in the love of God. You are not in the interaction of Him loving you and you loving Him back.

The truth is – you can't actually love God – you can only love Him back. You can only reciprocate the love that He has for you. To speak of loving God is to speak of a mutual experience of being loved by Him and reciprocating that love back to Him. But if you claim to love God and yet hate your brother you are simply deceived. It is not true that you can love God and hate your brother or sister. If you are in the interaction of God loving you and you loving Him back, it will be impossible to feel anything but love for your brother or your sister. My friend and brother, Stephen Hill, has made a great statement of truth. He said, *"If you love God more than you have a revelation and experience of Him loving you, it is merely a religious affection."* That is so true. If we love without living in the reality of Him loving us first it is only our fleshly zeal. We can only rightly love God back. Any love we have for God and others is a response and an outflow of His love for us.

Let me say this: **Love energises love. Christianity is self-energised. You don't have to make yourself a Christian. If you surrender to real Christianity, Christianity will make you a Christian.**

Christianity is being in the flow of the love of God into your heart. When the love of God is flowing into your heart you will become everything a Christian can be. You will become everything a Christian should be. You will become everything a Christian wants to be. Automatically.

When His love flows into your heart you will be at peace inside – even if you don't have a retirement plan. If you are not experiencing Him loving you, then you will live in fear. If you are in Christianity, then you will be at peace. If you are experiencing

Him loving you, then you will tend to have joy. It is a very joyful thing to be loved and joy is the fruit of love. That is the meaning of the 'fruit of the Spirit.' If the Spirit is the love of God poured into your heart, then the fruit of that is what love produces in you - and love produces joy, love produces peace, love produces kindness, goodness, patience, self-control, and so on. The fruit here (spoken of in Galatians 5) is spoken of in the singular - it is 'fruit', not 'fruits'. The love of God poured into our hearts by the Holy Spirit produces all of these things in one hit. You can't have one that is weak and that you need to 'work on' - the love produces this fruit without qualification or exception.

I always struggled with the last one on the list - self-control. It seems to be negative in contrast to all the others, which are positive. I used to think - and people would use it on me - that 'self-control' is the capacity to control yourself, to rein in your overwhelming natural desires. People would say to me, "The Spirit gives you self-control, so control yourself!" I always understood self-control as being the discipline not to sin, as being a command to control the lusts and desires of the flesh. This is how I understand it now; it is self-determination. In other words, when love comes into your life, you will be free of any external control. You will live your life by the love on the inside of you. With the Spirit of God indwelling me I am now led by the Spirit. Even if they try to crucify me to try and stop me living that way, I am led by the Holy Spirit within me and that is what controls me. It isn't about sin. The Spirit of God determines where I will go and what I will do. He determines what I think and what I say. Nobody controls me. By the indwelling Spirit, I am self-determined.

I believe this is exactly what it means. If my life is determined by love within me, then my conclusion is this - Christianity is actually anarchy. I am free from having to obey the laws of my country - *but only* if I am walking in the interacting love of the Father for me and my love for Him. If love rules me, I don't even have to think about what the laws of my country are. Love automatically fulfills every law.

In conclusion, the love of the Father is the determining factor in your life. Use your interconnectedness with God the Father as a barometer of the atmosphere of your life. If I have really negative feelings towards people, the problem is not my feeling towards the person. The problem is that I have lost connectedness with the Father. When you find these things in your life, they are symptoms of the lost connection between you and the Father's love. *Come back to His love for you.* In everything come back to that, because it is His love that will give you peace, joy, patience or whatever you need. Some people say, "I really need to learn more patience." Well, you can't. Patience is an outcome of something else. Patience comes from a greater reality. When His love is poured into your heart and you have love for someone, you don't mind waiting. You will gladly wait for ten years, twenty years or more. You will wait until the end of your life. Abraham was given promises that were not fulfilled within his own lifetime. Some of the things that God has spoken over your life will not be fulfilled in your own life. They will be fulfilled in the lives of your children. Some of the prophecies that God has given to you will not be fulfilled - but if you believe them right through to the end they will be fulfilled in your children or your children's children - because prophecy goes on generation after generation. The prophecies to Abraham are still being fulfilled today but, according to Hebrews, he didn't see them fulfilled. Love will give you patience. Love will give you all these things.

Sometimes people say to me, "What can I do? What is there for me to do in the ministry?" My response to that question is generally this, "Just enjoy the Father loving you. If you keep enjoying His love being poured into your heart, somewhere along the way it will start overflowing out of you." If you want to do something with it, you will never get filled with it enough for it to be useable. But if you just allow Him to keep loving you and you grow in that love, the day will come when people will begin to ask you to share what has happened to you and what is going on in your life. You will begin to share, and as the love of God overflows from your heart, people will be blessed.

Never focus on what is coming out. Focus on what is coming in. If love keeps coming in it's only a matter of time until it begins to spill over. I like what Jack Frost used to say. He said that the inflow of the Father's love only has to reach the point of 51% and the seesaw will tilt the other way. You don't have to be filled to 99% before you affect others. All it takes is to reach an infilling of 51% for the tipping point to be reached. Enjoy receiving His love until that happens. The love of the Father encompasses everything that is Christian. It is the substance of the Gospel. I once thought it was one of the main truths of the gospel but now I see that *it is* the Gospel.

WHAT SONSHIP REALLY IS

Sonship is living in the Father's manifested love. Many people have turned sonship into something that *we* have to do or an attitude that *we* need to adopt. Sonship, however, is living in the experiential love of the Father and in intimate relationship with Him. It is in that place of receiving and experiencing His loving you. We have turned many things in Christianity into things that *we* must do. One of the primary questions asked by Christians is, "How do I do this? How do I walk as a son? How do I live in this love?" That makes no sense. Within a family it is the relationship that is the issue. A person is a son or a daughter by relationship. You will grow in sonship, not by having the right attitude towards God but by experiencing Him loving you - *only by experiencing Him loving you*. His love going into your heart will automatically bring you into maturity.

Love is stuff. Love is a substance. It is an emotional energy of eternal substantiveness. It is nothing less than the substance of God's life. It is a substance, which comes from God's heart and God's heart alone. No human being can give to you the love of God. This love is resident in the very heart of God. And when He pours that love into your heart, real stuff goes into you. When that substance goes into you, you *will* experience being loved. It's not about *believing* that He loves you; it's about *being loved* by Him.

That substance will automatically change your life. It will bring forth the fruit of the Spirit. It will manifest in the traits of *true* Christian character. It will manifest itself to those around you. That stuff will turn you into everything a Christian is meant to be. It says about Jesus in John 1:18:

> *No one has seen God at any time. The only begotten Son who is in the bosom of the Father, He has declared Him.*

Some people try to 'declare' God; they preach on Christian things without the experiential knowledge of the Father's bosom. As the Body of Christ matures, these ministries will become obsolete.

Jesus lived in the bosom of the Father, continuously experiencing the Father's heart of love for Him personally. He did not visit there once or twice or touch His Father's heart from time to time. He was *abiding* there - in the bosom of the Father.

The whole point of the existence of Fatherheart Ministries is to teach people how to continually experience this substance of the love of the Father coming out of His heart into ours. How do you mature in that? You get more and more filled with the love of the Father. The more that happens the more patient you will be, the more kind you will be. You *will* lay down your life for the sake of others. That love will fill you to the point of overflowing, and then the talents He has given you, the gifts of the Spirit made available to us all, and the ministries of the Spirit given to build the Body of Christ will flow with unprecedented effect and truly glorify our God and Father.

The key to Christianity is this: If we are to become competent at anything it is this one thing. *Learn to become an expert at receiving the substance of God the Father's love being poured into your heart.* We often quote the well-known verse, "Perfect love casts out fear," thinking it means that we will worry less if we believe enough that God loves us. No! Let me tell you: when you get full of this substance in your heart you won't have the *capacity* to worry anymore. It will be impossible for you to even think of what the concept of fear means. That is what sonship is. As we receive and keep on receiving this love into our hearts it will turn us into the exact likeness of Jesus.

We have already seen a tremendous outpouring of the love of God the Father but it has been little more than a splash compared to what is coming. Don't be satisfied until the love of the Father becomes resident inside you, changing you into the image of Jesus. It is His love, resident within you, that transforms you into a Christian.

When we put this book together we didn't know where to place this final chapter. We didn't know whether to put it first or last. My advice to you is this: now that you have read the whole book, go back and read it again, and you will understand it better.

I believe that we are living in a time of the restoration of the Gospel that Paul preached to the Galatians when they were believing another gospel, a gospel that was not good news. We are living in a time when God is restoring again what the Gospel actually is. We are rediscovering that ancient highway, so neglected for centuries. As we learn to live in the experiencing of the Father continually loving us we are eating from the Tree of Life and all the issues that pertain to real Christianity become automatic in our life's experience. Jesus secured the right for us to experience the same freedom that God Himself experiences. It is my hope and prayer that this book will set you again on that ancient road, carried by the dancing Holy Spirit, into the likeness of Jesus in the love of the Father.

An Invitation...

If you enjoyed reading this book we invite you to a Fatherheart Ministries 'A' School. Fatherheart Ministries 'A' Schools are a one week environment of the revelation of love.

The Two Goals of 'A' Schools are:
1. To give an opportunity for you to have a personal major experience of the love that God the Father has for you.
2. To give the strongest Biblical understanding possible of the place of the Father in the Christian life and walk.

During the school you will be introduced to the full perspective of the revelation of Father's love. Through revelatory insight and sound biblical teaching told through the lives of those that minister you will be exposed to a transforming message of Love, Life and Hope.

You will be given the opportunity to remove the main blockages to receiving Father's love and discover your heart as a true son or daughter. Jesus had the heart of a son to His Father. He lived in the presence of the love of the Father. John's Gospel tells us that everything that He said and did was what He saw and heard His Father doing. Jesus invites us to enter that world as brothers and sisters of Him the first born.

As we open our hearts Father pours His love into our hearts by the Holy Spirit. In a heart transformed by His love, true and lasting change will occur. After years of striving and perfomance many are finally finding the way home, to a place of rest and belonging.

To apply for an A School visit 'Schools & Events' at

www.fatherheart.net

Additional copies of this book and other resources
from Fatherheart Media are available at:

www.fatherheart.net/shop - New Zealand
www.fatherheartmedia.com - Europe
www.amazon.com - Paperback & Kindle versions

FATHERHEART MEDIA

PO BOX 1039
Taupo, 3330, New Zealand

Visit us at www.fatherheart.net

19056764R00118

Made in the USA
San Bernardino, CA
10 February 2015